The old-time pamphlet ethos is back, with some of the most challenging work being done today. Prickly Paradigm Press is devoted to giving serious authors free rein to say what's right and what's wrong about their disciplines and about the world, including what's never been said before. The result is intellectuals unbound, writing unconstrained and creative texts about meaningful matters.

"Long live Prickly Paradigm Press.... Long may its flaming pamphlets lift us from our complacency."
—Ian Hacking

Prickly Paradigm is marketed and distributed by The University of Chicago Press.

www.press.uchicago.edu

A list of current and future titles can be found on our website and at the back of this pamphlet.

www.prickly-paradigm.com

Executive Publisher
Marshall Sahlins

Publishers
Peter Sahlins
Ramona Naddaff
Seminary Co-op Bookstore

Editor
Matthew Engelke
info@prickly-paradigm.com

Design and layout by Daniel Murphy.

# The Jewish Question Again

# The Jewish Question Again

Edited by Joyce Dalsheim and Gregory Starrett

PRICKLY PARADIGM PRESS
CHICAGO

Prickly Paradigm Press, LLC
5629 South University Avenue
Chicago, IL 60637

www.prickly-paradigm.com

ISBN: 9781734643503
LCCN: 2020947394

Printed in the United States of America on acid-free paper.

# Contents

# Introduction:
# The Jewish Question, Again

Joyce Dalsheim and Gregory Starrett

The past resembles the future more than one drop of
water another.                    —Ibn Khaldun, 1377

אַל־תֹּאמַר מֶה הָיָה שֶׁהַיָּמִים הָרִאשֹׁנִים הָיוּ טוֹבִים מֵאֵלֶּה כִּי לֹא מֵחָכְמָה
שָׁאַלְתָּ עַל־זֶה:

(Do not say, "How was it that the former days were
better than these?" For not out of wisdom have you
asked concerning this.)          —Ecclesiastes 7:10

We have always already lived in times of recurrence, but
some of those times are especially striking. The return
of authoritarian nationalism to political respectability,
fresh waves of refugees turned away at border crossings
or crowded into fenced encampments across the globe,
and flashes of racist, xenophobic, and misogynistic
violence making headlines in the Western democracies
that were supposed to have transcended such acts; all
of these appear as the unwelcome return of a series of
rejected pasts.

Many of us have felt a sense of astonishment when faced with the sharp rightward swing of politics. Shock is displayed in popular demonstrations where people hold placards proclaiming, "I can't believe I'm still protesting this!" There is a sense of disbelief that certain ideas, practices, and policies have not been relegated to the dustbin of the past, but represent something like a "return of the repressed." Both the idea of return and the idea of repression lead us to ask again—now, still—about the ongoing relevance of the historical "Jewish question." That is, what is the place of "the Jew"—the minority, the relic, the rootless stranger, the exiled, the displaced, the immigrant, the diasporic—within the boundaries of the polis?

While often equated with antisemitism, the Jewish question was never exclusively about Jews. It was a contest over questions of faith and reason, loyalty to authority and community, the potential for human liberation, and the meaning and future of "Christendom," "Europe," and "the West," through a specific idiom of otherness. This book is part of an ongoing project that asks how such questions endure; that is, how are they bound up with time? Here we explore these questions in the form of multiple fragments of conversations that intersect each other and fold back on themselves in multiple ways. None of us is at all finished with these issues. Thinking through the politics of their recurrence, therefore, is increasingly urgent.

During another time of violence, displacement, and social reorientation—the period immediately following the collapse of the Roman Empire, sixteen centuries ago—Saint Augustine thought about how to find an anchor for the eternal truth of Christ in the chaotic temporality of the secular world. His long meditation on this question in *The City of God* found such an anchor in the Jews, who confirmed Christian truth by standing outside it. God had dispersed the Jews among every nation, with their ancient scriptures clearly foretelling Christ's mission. They stood as witnesses to Christian history, "lest perchance any one should say that the Christians have forged these prophecies."[1] The practical value of the Jews, although they themselves "have remained stationary in useless antiquity,"[2] lay specifically in their diaspora. Their role was to constitute a material contrast to the new "spiritual Israel" of the Church that superseded them, negating, preserving, and transcending their legacy.

Since that time, "the Jews" have embodied a long series of binary distinctions in European thought. What Augustine identified as the Jew's uncanny dual nature—stubborn traditionalism coexisting with cosmopolitan mobility—was perceived by later intellectuals as a frightening capacity to assimilate joined to an eternal racial essence, a volatile contradiction that interfered with the ability to think about national purity and cultural solidarity. From Augustine to Kant, Rousseau, and Herder, to Marx and Weber, through Arendt and the Frankfurt School, and on to Said, Derrida, and Ella Shohat, the question of the Jews and the meaning of their presence have formed a central part of the *longue durée* of the social and political philosophy of Europe and its Others. Both anthropologist Gelya Frank and historian Ronald Schechter have concluded independently that Jews have been, in Lévi-Strauss's terms, "good to think."[3]

As a result, classical social theory has been shaped largely by the way the Jewish question framed first Christian and then European identities.[4] The ideology of the modern nation-state made religious and ethnic differences nurtured in previous centuries into a new kind of problem. And that prompted new lines of scholarly inquiry, about everything from the impact of social environment and law on individual behavior to basic questions of how group membership works, how movement and residence might be regulated, how religion and state are connected, how human collectives are linked to place across geographical and temporal distance, and how identity categories overlap, conflict, intensify, or exclude each other.

Despite decades of theorization and critique, the patterns of exclusion and violence characteristic of ethnonationalism and racism—two of the multiple structures of difference that have shaped the Jewish question over recent centuries—are consistently reproduced in the very conceptual frameworks and practical projects that politicians, intellectuals, and activists propose as their solution. While scholars may insist on inquiring into the historical context of these structures, deconstructing enemy categories and revealing longer-term processes, it is not uncommon for theory to be abandoned in the name of praxis.[5] But abandoning such theoretical frameworks not only undermines our scholarly values, it also risks undermining the very goals of social and political praxis. When such praxis finds its way into scholarly associations, it is especially disheartening to witness, as deep historical context and critical theory vanish.

It took some time for the American Anthropological Association (AAA) to initiate formal discussions on questions of Palestine/Israel. AAA had longed welcomed member activism on issues such as indigeneity in Latin America and elsewhere, but this particular issue seemed too contentious. Ultimately, when the association did take it up, it did so in two ways. First, in the form of panels scheduled at its annual meetings to discuss the powerful grassroots movement for Boycott, Divestment, and Sanctions (BDS). And second, by constituting an official Task Force on AAA Engagement on Israel-Palestine. Ironically, the task force excluded any scholar with primary expertise in the area, a decision that would have been unthinkable had the group been focused on any other region. And just as unfortunately, the discussions focused on BDS often narrowed into bare, utilitarian "pro" and "con" positions. Each "side"—and there were only two possible sides—appealed to established cultural values of liberation, human rights, or academic freedom to recruit supporters for their cause.

Dissatisfied with the limited frameworks of the profession's discussion, Joyce Dalsheim spoke with Jonathan Boyarin, who suggested it might be time to reconsider the Jewish question. As a result, we organized an Executive Program Committee invited roundtable at the 2015 AAA annual meeting, in Denver, titled "The Jewish Question Again: Palestine, Europe, and the Elementary Structures of Expulsion," to examine some of the broader theoretical issues and conceptual histories that seemed to have been lost and forgotten in much of AAA's framing of the issue. With Europe provincialized in the wake of the emergence of postcolonial studies, the Jewish question continues to raise issues. These issues include secularism and citizenship, minorities and subaltern groups, migrants and refugees, and displacement and identity, far beyond the specific identities of Jew and Arab, Muslim and Jew. The Jewish question continues to problematize the quest for liberation through sovereignty in the form of the modern nation-state, whether in the states currently constituting "Europe" or in the state of Israel, which is self-consciously modeled on them.

But at the panel itself, we were scolded sharply by members of the audience, particularly by younger scholars from Europe. They perceived the phrase "the Jewish Question Again" as inherently antisemitic and possibly an attempt to propose or revive some "new kind of 'Solution'" to the problem, either in Europe or in Palestine. Some were angry that we were discussing the issue at all and were incredulous that the AAA would sponsor and condone such a round-table, or even allow us to utter out loud the phrase "the Jewish Question." Many were so shaken by the title of the panel that they apparently could not hear what the panelists said, including Gil Anidjar's pointed observation that the Jewish question was now in essence Europe's "Muslim question," and had all along informed the very distinction between Jew and Arab that was at stake in the debates about Palestine. And so, dear reader, we hope that you will take a deep breath and listen more patiently.

Some audience members at that 2015 panel were unwilling or unable to think back further than the 1930s, or beyond the idea of antisemitism specifically, to consider the central role that Jewish histories have played in structuring the way Euro-American traditions of thought and practices of estrangement frame the world. For them, such deep histories appear to have been truncated by a peculiar kind of periodization. If one of the virtues of postcolonial and critical traditions of scholarship is the quest for alternative conceptualizations of difference that do not emerge from the white, Western, capitalist episteme, it seems curious that the historical Jewish question has been largely absent from these conversations.

What often appears instead in such periodizations is an implicit assumption that hierarchies of difference replace and eliminate one another over time. If the Jew and the Muslim defined and ensured the status of the Christian in medieval Europe, things began to change with the beginnings of European exploration in the Americas, Africa, and the Pacific; with plantation capitalism, the Atlantic slave trade, and settler colonization. New Others, including the Black and the Indian, came to provide new means by which European Christians might through contrast understand their own humanity and define their local concerns. Robert Launay's insightful recent book, *Savages, Romans, and Despots*, for example, shows how, from the fourteenth century,

> characterizations of non-Europeans have figured, sometimes centrally and sometimes peripherally, in polemical arguments of concern primarily—sometimes exclusively—to Europeans: arguments about politics, religion, history, even art and literature ... But the stakes have been the domination not necessarily of Europeans over non-Europeans, but of the claims of one group of Europeans—a religious community, a

political faction, an intellectual clique—over another. Representations of non-Europeans have been mobilized as tools for thinking and arguing about purely European issues.[6]

Providing such tools has been one of the roles traditionally played—from ancient times well into the twentieth century—by the already well-known figure of the Jew in Christian thought. But if Jews sometimes count as just another group of white elites and imperialists now, it might seem reasonable to ignore the lessons that their own history of subalterity teaches us about difference and its patterns of repetition over the long term. For example, the forced conversion of medieval and early modern Jews was sometimes considered necessary for them to become part of Europe. But those conversions were never taken entirely seriously by Christians, who often doubted the converts' sincerity and increasingly perceived the Jews as eternally and hereditarily alien. Likewise, the forced conversion of native peoples and enslaved Africans in the Americas was also always suspect, and never quite allowed them to be considered full brothers in Christ. Their difference was construed as the apparent material reality of an eternal racial essence and maintained by brutal systems of land and labor expropriation. A universalist view of human nature wherein difference and virtue were defined by movements of the will, and through which one could choose to become a new person, had given way to an essentialist notion of human difference in which the improvement of the soul could never erase the perfidy of origin.

That contrast itself, between race and conscience or between body and soul, replays ancient Christian claims about the contrast between Jewish and Christian essence, which revolved around distinctions between materiality and spirituality. It also participates in the Christian effort to separate and extract the notion of "Judaism" as a "religion" from the living practices of Jews as a people or a nation.[7] This in turn distinguishes the possibility of individual thought and practice from the fact of community membership, and separates law from piety. Such repetitions illustrate how patterns of precarity and suspicion, distinction and similarity, experience and abstraction, endure and transform themselves through time in different registers and with different implications.

Jewish differences and histories were among the roots and sources of our contemporary intellectual means of constructing and sorting out the idea of difference itself, including such concepts as religion, tribe, ethnicity, race, nation, diaspora, and citizenship. Scholars in anthropology, cultural studies, and other fields have inherited the concern for defining, elaborating, managing, or deconstructing categorizations of difference, sometimes critiquing and sometimes furthering the work such categories perform. Forgetting the theological and political roots of these ideas makes it difficult to discuss issues of global significance without entrenching the systems of identity, distinction, and solidarity that such theory was developed not merely to describe, critique, and analyze, but to suppress or justify.

Although we currently embrace the productivity of excluded identity positions for the development of critical theory, Jewishness is not generally seen as one

of those productive identities. Jews, historically foundational to Euro-American understandings of belonging
and exclusion, can no longer comfortably be thought
of as subaltern. There are, of course, exceptions to
this general rule, studies that engage seriously with
Jewish historical experience in Europe as a model
of or a source for thinking about other cases. These
include, for example, Aamir Mufti's *Enlightenment in
the Colony* (2007), Faisal Devji's *Muslim Zion* (2013),
Mayanthi Fernando's *The Republic Unsettled* (2014),
Saba Mahmood's *Religious Difference in a Secular Age*
(2015), Dorian Bell's *Globalizing Race* (2018), and
perhaps, from the other side of the mirror, Nadia Abu
El-Haj's *The Genealogical Science* (2012). Each of these
thinks with the history of the Jewish question in order
to illuminate issues of racialization, ethnonationalism,
religion, and claims to indigeneity in the colonial and
postcolonial world. That all these works are so recent
might indicate something of a turning point in contemporary scholarship.

There is an additional sense, though, in which
the historical and still disputed subaltern position of
Jews enters into the issue of scholarship. That is in the
potential for bringing certain styles of Jewish thought
into the anthropology of the present.

Following our AAA panel in Denver, in 2015,
we sought support for a stand-alone interdisciplinary
conference to advance the conversation that had begun
there. But even after the reappearance of Nazis and
Klansmen in Charlottesville, Virginia, in August 2017,
we were unable to convince reviewers on foundation
funding panels that it was a worthwhile exercise. In
spring 2018, however, Jonathan Boyarin, who had

participated in the Denver panel, was able to secure generous funding for a weekend workshop on the Jewish question, sponsored by the Jewish Studies Program and the Society for the Humanities at Cornell University, adding perspectives from across the humanities and beyond. We are deeply grateful for his inspiration, his efforts on behalf of this project, and for his specific contributions to this conversation.

This volume contains four chapters that engage with some of the themes that arose in Denver and at Cornell. We present them here as fragments of longer and ongoing discussions that, like "thinking in Jewish" more generally,[8] demonstrate the need for constant attention and, much like the process of studying Talmud, encourage thinking and rethinking the same sorts of problems again, still.

Holly Case sketches the history of how the "Jewish question" as a named intellectual object emerged in the nineteenth century as part of "the age of questions." She provides a glimpse into how the Jewish question was and was not like those other questions. One of the things that made the Jewish question "real" was its protean character, its chronic redefinition of focus. Such questions "appeared with a feint, for at the moment they were first invoked they were also assigned a long history" that begged for solutions that seemed long overdue. The specific solutions proposed turned on the identity of the questioner, but all were expressed in terms of a characteristic nineteenth-century style of thought: an opposition to whatever was taken as the status quo, and a sense of certainty that a radical change in the social order (whether progressive or reactionary) was urgently needed. "Those who spoke in the form of questions," Case writes, "did so generally to call for sweeping changes in domestic policy, the international order, or both."

The sense that questions are catalysts for rapid and transformative change contrasts with the temporal rhythm outlined in the dialogue between Jonathan Boyarin and Martin Land. The pair write of a very different intellectual style, one characteristic of Talmud scholarship, which might inform what they call a Jewish anthropology of the present. It is a style in which acknowledgment of the integrity or authority of a textual tradition allows one to claim the freedom "to seriously question the validity of widely accepted conclusions without fear of causing the entire superstructure to collapse." Questions are understood to recur; to revisit, enrich, and even reverse common understandings without necessarily transforming them. But these rethinkings are not generally expected to result in conclusions to be taken as final.

Starrett and Dalsheim—the similarly dialogic structure of whose chapter was coincidental—also discuss the idea of recurrence. We focus on the widespread astonishment among intellectuals and activists when previously rejected elements of our own political past—racism, antisemitism, misogyny, xenophobia—seemed to rise from the graveyard of history. If people were surprised that the promise of social and moral progress has not rid us of these curses, we suggest that the problem is not with the reality we are currently experiencing. The problem is that the idea of "progress"—as Walter Benjamin pointed out so long ago—is just bad theory. In order to become better prepared for the present we need to think about the kinds of patterned recurrences illustrated by the Jewish question in both its senses: as a way of thinking about deep empirical histories of difference and injustice, and as a way of thinking about the constant duty to reexamine one's own tradition.

Gil Anidjar brings it all back to now—but also then—in his meditation on the "Muslim/Arab question," which is also still, again, the Jewish question. Anidjar calls on the work of Houria Bouteldja, whose critical thinking emerges from an indigenous anticolonial perspective. If, as Bouteldja proposes, the Jews are the embattled buffer between white Christianity and the world's colonized masses, then their histories and prospects might be reframed "to draw a common future from a conception of history that insists on separations." Anidjar thus builds on and reinforces his own previous work interrogating the twin processes of race and religion that have come to naturalize the Jew and the Arab as polarized identities, processes that often fade into the background of current debates.

Like the Jewish question itself—which is also the Muslim question, the question of the stranger, the outsider, the enemy, the Other—the essays in this book never quite end. Anidjar concludes with an open question, Starrett and Dalsheim end in an ellipsis, and Boyarin and Land finish with an unfinished proposal for an anthropology of a present that is constantly in motion. Case comes closest to a narrative conclusion, writing that after all the grand urgent questions of the nineteenth century, no one really thinks about these issues in quite that sense anymore. After the Second World War, she writes, the Jewish question "shared with the other grand questions of the nineteenth century a last journey into semi-oblivion wherein it is mainly scholars who continue to speak and write of them."

Scholars, yes. But we might add "fanatics." The recurrence of a politics that takes the Jewish question seriously again as a means of mobilization requires a way of thinking that is perhaps best expressed by the rabbi in Joann Sfar's marvelous graphic novel, *The Rabbi's Cat*: "Western thought," the rabbi says, "works by thesis, antithesis, synthesis, while Judaism goes thesis, antithesis, antithesis, antithesis ..."

# 2
# The Jewish Question
# in the Age of Questions

Holly Case

It's hard to add anything new to the writing on the "Jewish question." There are works on "the Jewish question in Poland," on "Freud's Jewish question," and on the relationship between the "Jewish question" and the "woman question." It seems that everyone, from Marx to Freud to Dostoevsky to Goebbels to Sartre, had something to say about the "Jewish question." The American philosopher Richard Bernstein recalls that "when I was a teenager growing up in Brooklyn (during the Second World War), there were many local jokes about 'the Jewish question.' 'The Jewish question and ————' was a formula where one could simply, imaginatively fill in the blank. ... For example, 'The Jewish question and the Brooklyn Dodgers.'"[1]

And that was before the "Jewish question" became a scholarly preoccupation. It is therefore difficult for us to stifle an intellectual yawn upon seeing the phrase, and not because it has failed to elicit any feeling or enthusiasm. On the contrary. In fact, it is in part the very frenzied and dogged passion that the question has evoked that has contributed to its status as a pervasive, yet somehow also outmoded strain of historical inquiry.

The Jewish question was one of a great many questions that appeared in the nineteenth century during the period I call "the age of questions."[2] Starting in the early 1800s were born the corn, bullion, and population questions. Soon there was also a Polish question, then Eastern, slavery, woman, and labor (worker) questions. Over the course of the first half of the nineteenth century, these questions would be conglomerated into still broader ones—the European, nationality, social, and agrarian questions, for example—even as they also fractured into countless smaller ones (like the Macedonian and Schleswig-Holstein questions), and made their way into various fields of human endeavor (like the cotton and sugar questions, for example). So dense was the pamphleteering mania around "questions" that in 1893 Tolstoy wrote: "I constantly receive from all kinds of authors all kinds of pamphlets, and frequently books. ... One has definitely settled the question of Christian gnoseology ... a third has settled the social question, a fourth—the political question, a fifth—the Eastern question."[3] Even Tolstoy himself shared his views on the "Eastern question" through the character of Levin in the last segment of *Anna Karenina.*[4]

Some features of the Jewish question make it unique among other "questions," but the reflexive passion and exasperation it has inspired is not one of them. Most if not all of these questions periodically drove commentators to ecstasies of shrill indignation, frustration, and ennui. Examining the markings and violence done to written sources on the "Polish question," for example, is proof enough that the phrase touched many a nerve: whole chapters torn with apparent fury out of books, and plenty of shrill marginalia ("Hypocrisy!" "Not for the Poles!"). And there is a joke—with many variations—that goes something like this: At an international essay competition on the subject of elephants, "the Englishman wrote 'Elephants I Have Shot'; the American wrote 'Bigger and Better Elephants'; the Frenchman wrote 'L'Eléphante et Ses Amours'; the Pole wrote 'The Elephant and the Polish Question.'"[5] You will even find the phrase "Słoń a sprawa polska" (The elephant and the Polish question) on Polish Wikipedia.

In his epic history of Poland, *God's Playground: 1795 to the Present*, Norman Davies wrote that, "For 150 years, the Polish Question was a conundrum that could not be solved, a circle that could never be squared. In that time, it generated mountains of archival material and oceans of secondary literature. For the historian of Poland, however, the Polish Question is a singularly barren subject."[6]

Compare this to the effect the so-called Eastern question had on commentators of the nineteenth century. One author writing in an evening newspaper in 1881 longed for the "termination" of "this tedious Eastern Question,"[7] and a poem in an 1883 issue of London's *Mayfair Magazine* includes a comic-pathetic line declaring that "the 'Eastern Question' is a bore."[8] Alexis de Tocqueville compared engagement with the Eastern question to "banging one's head against the wall."[9] "The Eastern question," wrote the Turkish writer

Namık Kemal, "is the name of those calamities of politics that have, for two centuries, been feared in the manner of volcanoes that erupt with fire at the least desirable time and change the face of the earth with an earthquake of misfortunes."[10] In Modern Greek, the phrase "You've made an Eastern question (out of it)" is a common idiom meaning "You've made a mountain out of a molehill."

Another feature that the Jewish question shares with other questions is that, by "question," those writing about and on it generally mean "problem." Bruno Bauer's 1843 *Die Judenfrage* (The Jewish question), for example, is generally translated as "The Jewish Problem."[11] As historian Mary Gluck writes, "It is customary to put quotation marks around the Jewish question, since it was not so much a question as an exclusionary discourse about Jewish citizenship and national identity."[12]

The etymology of "question" in several languages goes back to Latin. Its twelfth-century Middle-French and Anglo-Norman meanings included "query, inquiry" as well as "problem or topic which is under discussion or which must be investigated."[13] These two meanings cohabitate in the words for "question" in French, German, Russian, and most of the other European languages. The linking of questions to solutions is apparent in English in the sixteenth century. For the most part, nineteenth-century questions were synonymous with problems, which rhetorically called for solutions rather than answers or opinions. The implications of this slippage are manifold.

In his memoir, the late critic and philosopher Christopher Hitchens wrote that "Of course one is flirting with calamity in phrasing things this way, as I learned in school when the Irish question was discussed by some masters as the Irish 'problem.' Again, the word 'solution' can be as neutral as the words 'question' or 'problem,' but once one has defined a people or a nation as such, the search for a resolution can become a yearning for the conclusive. *Endlösung*: the final solution."[14]

And though we might think the idea of a "final solution" adheres uniquely to the Jewish question, that is not the case, either. "With the final solution of the Eastern question," Dostoevsky wrote in 1876, "all other political strife in Europe will be terminated … The formula—'the Eastern question'—comprises, perhaps unknowingly to itself, all other political questions, perplexities and prejudices of Europe."[15] Indeed, thinking in formulas and "final solutions" was a common feature of the century of questions. In a speech delivered by Napoléon III to the French Chamber of Deputies on the occasion of the opening of the legislative session in November 1863, the emperor spoke of the "sugar question" as demanding a "final solution."

There are a lot of questions a historian might pose about the Jewish question in light of these parallels. One could ask: How did they come about? Or, given the parallels, what, then, is unique about the Jewish question? I have some tentative answers to these questions, but first I would like to address a different one, namely: What does the "Jewish question" tell us about the "age of questions" more generally?

Let's begin at the beginning. Jewish historian Jacob Toury notes that although there were tangential semantic near misses during the revolutionary period in France, "a *question juive* did not emerge." He believes this fact is indicative that "neither a tense social situation nor party politics, nor even ideological altercations between conservatism and liberalism were at the root of the later concept of a 'Jewish Question.'"[16] Ultimately he places the origins of the slogan in the 1830s, concluding that "the 'Jewish question' as a slogan did not take roots until it had established itself as an anti-Jewish battle-cry," namely with two long essays published in 1838 in German titled *Die Jüdische Frage*.[17] The anonymous author of the essays argued that, on the basis of their essentially alien characteristics, Jews should not be given political equality in Prussia. A small flurry of publications in 1842 in Germany used the term *Judenfrage*, all to argue against full and immediate equality. Toury concludes that "the slogan *Judenfrage* ... initiated a new phase in the development of anti-Jewish bias. Its ideological connotations foreshadowed the development of those forms of antisemitism that became rampant in Western Europe at the end of the nineteenth century."[18] Therefore, "Jews," he writes, "could not concede the existence of a 'Jewish question' in the same sense as their adversaries," one that was already loaded with prejudice against them.[19]

The perspective changes when one considers the Jewish question not in isolation, in terms of a trajectory of European Jewish history toward the Holocaust, but as one of many questions that came into being around the 1830s. Germany does not appear to have been the birthplace of the Jewish question, as Toury implies. One earlier reference to the "Jewish question," from 1830 (more than a decade before the famous exchange on the subject between Bruno

Bauer and Karl Marx), cites the efforts of letter writers to the London *Times* to influence public opinion in advance of the debate of legislation relating to Jews in Parliament. "We must decline the insertion of any of the numerous letters on the Jewish question, about to be decided by Parliament," we read in a brief notice "To Correspondents" from April 23 of that year.[20] The notice suggests that there already existed some sort of understanding as to what the "Jewish question" referred to, and a fair amount of agitation if a flood of letters on the subject had been received.

Toury's conclusion that the "Jewish question" was loaded against Jews had earlier precedents. In the words of the Hungarian communist Erik Molnár, writing in 1946, there had long been many voices declaring that there *was no Jewish question*, by which they meant that "the Jewish question was an artificial creation of politically motivated demagoguery. Without antisemitic propaganda no one would speak of a Jewish question."[21] It is telling, for example, that the *Encyclopaedia Judaica* does not contain an entry for the "Jewish question," while *Antisemitism: A Historical Encyclopedia of Prejudice and Persecution* does.[22]

The notion that bias was built into the very question was not unique to the Jewish question. In the words of an Ottoman statesman in Benjamin Disraeli's 1847 novel *Tancred; or, The New Crusade*, "For my part, it seems to me that your Eastern question is a great imbroglio that only exists in the cabinets of diplomatists. Why should there be any Eastern question? All is very well as it is."[23] The fictional character's outburst matches another one famously uttered by the (real) Austrian diplomat Anton von Prokesch-Osten: "In

Turkey there is no Eastern question!" Such ideas were frequently overlaid by sardonic commentary on the pervasiveness of "imaginary" questions. "I verily believe that there is no Eastern Question at all," declares a character in a satirical piece by a British journalist from 1877, "but that the entire thing is an invention got up and maintained by subscription among our newspapers at home, in order to increase their circulation."[24]

The "Eastern question" makes for an especially interesting comparison. The Ottoman Empire might be considered the geopolitical counterpart of the Jews insofar as even its staunchest defenders could be seen as "anti-Turkish" in the same way that defenders of Jewish emancipation—from Bauer to Marx to Dostoevsky to Sartre—have been considered antisemitic.

So was the "Jewish question" *real* after all? Did it refer to some definable phenomenon or set of political and social relations agreed upon by commentators of the time and since? To the first I would say yes, the question was real; to the second, no. The question was real in that it bore the characteristics of most other questions of the time, but one of the characteristics that made it a real *question* was that it was chronically redefined. This last assertion requires some explanation.

The interrogative is as old as language. Indeed, "questions" are an essential element of the Socratic method. The scholastics of the late medieval and early modern period had their "quæstio(nes)," catechisms worked through posing questions that set up scriptural answers, and the national academies that sprang up throughout Europe in the seventeenth and eighteenth centuries had their question competitions. But the kind of question that emerged in the nineteenth century was something new, the shorthand for which might be given as "the x question."

A peculiar feature of these questions is that their origins are consistently obscured by the rhetorical modes in which they were discussed. Questions appeared with a feint, for at the moment they were first invoked they were also assigned a long history. This made them seem older than they actually were. For example, though the earliest source I have located that makes reference to the "Jewish question" is the London *Times* notice from 1830, many commentators on the Jewish question have traced its origins as far back as the very origins of Judaism.[25] Although the appearance of the "Eastern question" in state correspondence and published sources dates to the 1820s and 1830s, most works on it trace its origins back at least to the emergence of czarist Russia as a factor in determining the future of the Ottoman Empire within the European state system, with the Russo-Turkish war of 1768–74 and the subsequent treaty of Küçük Kaynarca, of 1774. A number of historians have gone farther back still, to the Ottoman expansion into southeastern Europe in the fourteenth and fifteenth centuries.

So why the backdating? One reason is that, although the slogan was new, the issues being discussed under the slogan often were not. More importantly, however, backdating had the effect of lending questions an aura of urgency, that it was "high time" to address the question, that redress was indeed "overdue." "The misery of the Jews is an anachronism," wrote Theodor Herzl in *The Jewish State*, in 1896.[26] This sense of urgency brings to mind another feature the Jewish question shares with others of the time, and that is that it was discussed in a genre I would generally call irritative, or "status-quo allergic"—a mood of agitation bordering on the pathological.

In 1879, the German historian Heinrich von Treitschke, calling on Jews to assimilate, wrote of how "anti-Semitic societies are formed, the 'Jewish question' is discussed in noisy meetings, a flood of anti-Semitic pamphlets appears on the market. There is only too much of dirt and brutality in these doings ..."[27] Three years later, the Russian Jewish physician Leon Pinsker wrote that "The age-old problem of the Jewish Question is causing emotions to run high today, as it has over the ages. Like the quadrature of the circle, it is an unsolved problem, but unlike it, it remains the burning question of the day."[28]

"When did the 'Jewish question' leap on my back?" wrote the Russian dramatist Leonid Andreyev during the First World War. "I don't know. I was born with it and under it. From the very moment I assumed a conscious attitude towards life until this very day I have lived in its noisome atmosphere, breathed in the poisoned air which surrounds all these 'problems,' all these dark, harrowing alogisms, unbearable to the intellect."[29] Other questions also seemed to produce a similarly involuntary, infectious distress. An 1834 book by the German Mennonite preacher Leonhard Weydmann criticized the "zeal" and "impatience," the "confusion of concepts and tangling of relations" that accompanied the "questions being discussed in our tumultuous time," which were essentially about the "desire and endeavor to change the existing [system]."[30] Given this, "There are few positions more embarrassing," according to the conservative Marquess of Salisbury, writing on the

Polish question in April 1863, "than that of men who hold moderate opinions in regard to questions upon which excitement is running high."[31]

What Weydmann correctly understood was that those who spoke in the form of questions did so generally to call for sweeping changes in domestic policy, the international order, or both. This might cause one to conclude that most such commentators were progressive. And indeed, there were many individuals advocating for various forms of emancipation among early querists. But they did not own "the *x* question" formulation, nor were they the only forces pushing for change. Weydmann—a traditionalist and religious conservative—is a prime example. Even *he* wanted radical change—change *back* to the way things had been before the catastrophic French Revolution. Indeed, unless we want to count individuals like Herzl, Houston Stewart Chamberlain, and Goebbels as progressives, the Jewish question serves as an important and clear corrective to common assumptions about the progressive and emancipationist drive behind the *x* question phenomenon more generally.

Part of the confusion around this point may stem from the assumption that people who abhor the status quo and want radical change are progressives. Through the nineteenth century up to the Second World War, however, this category of "status-quo allergic" included just about everyone, and the tone and structure of *x* questions emphasizes this.

As with many other period questions, the standard (if not universal) format of interventions on the Jewish question was often as follows: they begin like an undergraduate history paper (with a phrase like

"Since the dawn of time ...") ; then follows some claim to the uniqueness of the way the "question" is being framed in the present intervention, often accompanied by an assertion that the question has hitherto been incorrectly or hazily defined, that you can only glean the proper solution when you frame the question correctly, and that you must frame it *this way* if you are to reach a true understanding of the problem; and from there the analysis proceeds to the much-awaited "solution." Bauer's text on the *Judenfrage* works more or less like this, as does Marx's, Herzl's, the rabbi Henry Berkowitz's, and so on. (Never mind that the "solutions" proposed are—respectively—political emancipation on condition of the Jews relinquishing their faith, total transformation of the social and economic order, the creation of a "Jewish state," and a return to the principles put forward by Moses.) The author of a hefty pair of volumes on the "Jewish question" from 1980, Alex Bein, took a similar approach, though merely to historicize rather than with the aim of offering a "solution." In the introductory chapter, he put forward a number of definitions offered over time, and then himself defined the "Jewish question" as "the problem of the existence of the Jews among the nations," concluding that "Even this (provisional and crude) characterization of the Jewish question establishes that we are here dealing with a unique problem for which no real parallels can be found."[32] What is unique—and indeed intriguingly ahistorical—about Bein's assertion is the claim of uniqueness, for it was not until after the Second World War that commentators on the "Jewish question" started to regularly and self-consciously isolate it from the other "questions" of the time. The reasons for that are in part obvious, but in part obscure.

"The Final Solution" was shorthand for the "final solution to the Jewish question." After 1945 there was a sharp falloff in prescriptive treatments of "questions," one that continues more or less to this day. We don't really speak in "questions" anymore. Some have lingered, like the "German question" and the "Kurdish question," and occasionally the ghost of the "Eastern question" will reappear, or Putin will refer to the "Ukrainian question" and commentators will remark on how he has reverted to nineteenth-century thinking. But the "Final Solution" undeniably gave questions in general a bad name. Where the "question" once stood we now see words like "issue," "problem," "situation," or "crisis." And lest we think the "*x* problem" has taken the place of the "*x* question," it is worth noting that the formulation is now generally flipped, as well—"the problem of global warming" rather than the "global warming/climate problem," or "the problem of inequality," or "the crisis in Syria," the "situation in Ukraine," and so on.

We are, in general, much more contextual and temporally conservative ("crisis" and "situation" imply something relatively brief rather than protracted, as "question" can) in our discussion of contemporary concerns. In short, we make very few claims to universality—either in temporal or spatial terms—for even the most universal-seeming issues, such as inequality and climate change.

Things were different in the nineteenth century, when questions were eagerly universalized or internationalized. In 1892, the Italian writer Edmondo de

Amicis told a group of students at the University of Turin: "Don't listen to those who claim that the social question is only a question for industrial and agricultural workers ... No, it is a question for everyone." All classes are affected by it, he intoned, including the middle class.[33] Similarly, the Jewish question was cast as not just a problem for Jews, but as *everyone's* problem, and insofar as it was everyone's problem, its ultimate solution would redound to everyone's benefit. This was true regardless of whether the commentator was for or against emancipation.

In offering the "Jewish state" as "an inescapable conclusion," the necessary solution to the Jewish question, Herzl declared that "The world will be freed by our liberty, enriched by our wealth, magnified by our greatness. And whatever we attempt there to accomplish for our own welfare, will react powerfully and beneficially for the good of humanity."[34] Polish writer and nationalist activist Stephanie Laudyn (Stefanja Laudynowa), in *A World Problem: Jews—Poland—Humanity* (1920), wrote: "In studying the question, I have realized that the relation of the Jews in regard to Poland is exactly the same as their relations to the world at large. For that reason, the problem at issue intimately concerns other nations; in fact, affects their creeds, their ideals and aspirations."[35] And in 1946, in the immediate aftermath of the Holocaust, the Marxist theorist of revolution Ernest Mandel (a.k.a. Ernest Germain) wrote that "if the Jewish tragedy is only the symbol and to a certain measure the 'mirror of the future' for humanity, the only way out which still remains open to humanity is at the same time the solution of the Jewish question."[36]

So it was that the effects of the problem and solution were cast in terms of broad, even universal sweep. But the Jewish question was also concretely and self-consciously tied to other questions of the period in terms of conceptualization, manifestation, and solution. These parallels could take the form of *tu quoque* claims, which sought to excuse persecution on the grounds that "you also do this!" In 1902, for example, the Romanian minister of foreign affairs Ioan Lahovary compared the "Jewish question" in Romania to the "Algerian question" for France and the "Chinese question in California," arguing that "an immediate and radical solution is impossible. England, rich and powerful though she is, has not yet been able to solve the Irish question."[37]

More commonly, however, the claim was that the Jewish question bore similarities to other questions and could thus be solved as they had been solved. In 1882 a clergyman by the name of Walter Scott spoke of the links between the Eastern question and the Jewish question:

> Has a final settlement of the Eastern Question been arrived at? ... To hope for a final solution of the Eastern Question from the Berlin or any other Conference is a sad delusion ... The longer we reflect on this great question, the more carefully we examine it in light of the ever-living and abiding Word of God, we are perfectly satisfied that it is the Jewish and not merely the Eastern Question, that it directly concerns the Jew and not the Turk or the Muscovite, that it will be finally settled by Christ at His second Advent, and neither in Berlin nor in Constantinople, but at Jerusalem, and that

the result of all will be the full and glorious triumph of the Jewish people, and their headship over the nations under the personal reign of the Messiah."[38]

With a very different solution in view, Louis Brandeis wrote, in 1915, that "The Zionist movement is idealistic, but it is also essentially practical. It seeks to realize that hope; to make the dream of a Jewish life in a Jewish land come true as other great dreams of the world have been realized, by men working with devotion, intelligence, and self-sacrifice." Brandeis then suggested that the Jewish question might be solved the same way the Italian, Bulgarian, Greek, and Serbian questions had been—with national independence and statehood.[39] And the German political scientist Adolf Grabowsky, writing on the "Polish question" in December 1915, referred to the *Fragenbündel* (bundle of questions) that needed to be "sifted through and sorted out." The Polish question, Grabowski wrote, could—as part of a *Fragenbündel* with the Jewish question—find some common solution.[40] Hitler and his European allies were also question bundlers, who cast the "Final Solution" as part of a broader agenda to "solve" a great mass of other questions. One of National Socialism's prime objectives, Hitler said, was to "resolve all suspended questions in such a manner that another conflict cannot emerge, at least for the foreseeable future."[41]

After the Second World War this conception of the Jewish question as something that could and should be bundled with other questions came under mounting critique. The American founder of the Trotskyist movement, Albert Gates, writing in 1947 on "The Jewish Problem after Hitler," complained that the Fourth International had undertaken the "dreary reaffirmation of old ideas and programs accompanied by the repetitious explanation that 'there is no reason to change our position,' since 'there is nothing new in the situation,'" conflating "the Russian question, the national question and the Jewish question." Gates, by contrast, felt that "The Jewish problem today is so different qualitatively from the past, that it is almost entirely a new one demanding new solutions."[42]

In short, the Jewish question became unmoored from the other questions at more or less the same moment that it died as a slogan calling for prescriptive solutions. Hardly coincidentally, its passing also happened at roughly the same time that many other questions of the age slipped into relative obscurity. Thus the Jewish question shared with the other grand questions of the nineteenth century a last journey into semi-oblivion wherein it is mainly scholars who continue to speak and write of them.

# 3

# A Jewish Anthropology of the Present; or, The History of the Jewish Question as a Nightmare from Which We Will Never Awaken

Jonathan Boyarin and Martin Land

*Dear Reader: What follows is a segment of an ongoing if intermittent conversation between two old friends about the relations among Jewishness, politics, and time. This particular segment turns on the possible links between an analysis of human mortality grounded in traditional Jewish discourse, on the one hand, and the challenge to Jewish identity posed by the vision of a future without redemption, on the other.*

**Jonathan Boyarin (JB):** Beyond the critique of progress and beyond even what (I just learned a few days ago) has been identified as "neofinalism," how can or should we be thinking temporally about the relations between Jewishness and human consciousness? Without collapsing all of what we persist in calling "history" into just one damn thing after another or, what amounts to the same thing, a persistent nightmare or even, *pace* Benjamin, an ever-growing pile of wreckage, is there still to be found somehow in the poetics of Jewishness alternative resources for thinking *now* without losing a sense of responsibility for what we still call "the past" and "the future?" Or is that just another desperate attempt to evade once again our complicity?

**Martin Land (ML):** To complicate relations among varieties of Jewishness and human consciousness with yet another perspective, physics reminds us that to specify a now already presupposes an elaborate conception of past and future. We may avoid progress, teleology, and essence, but to speak of chronology leaves us responsible for thinking about the causality so implied. And so I am sympathetic to Raymond Ruyer's goal in *Neofinalism* (if not the result): "the freedom to accomplish a task that may be judged successful or not."[1] To reject the possibility of judgment, and thereby deny the existence of causal relations, is a symptom common to the spoken forms of that ever-growing pile of wreckage.

In a pair of articles about #MeToo in the *New Yorker* some months ago, Masha Gessen expressed concern that the laudable flood of condemnations of sexual harassment could become a familiar American sex panic that may ultimately undermine women's agency.[2] She wrote that she perhaps sees these issues more clearly as an immigrant, a woman, and a lesbian. And I immediately thought, "and a Jew." Yes, that marginality and intellectual creativity thing again. But aside from the absence of Augustinian revulsion toward sex, what is Jewish about this? I was reminded of the notion that Christians reason by allegory, while Jews reason by analogy. Gessen seems to recognize an element of allegory and, by posing an analogy, make a judgment.

Please elaborate on your suggestion that thinking now should be different from thinking in some other way. Is it simply too radical at this moment to suggest that judgment is possible without reference to "essence" or "teleology," and that to make a judgment is not necessarily to be judgmental? Must judgment imply substitution of the intersubjective by the radically subjective? Whether deep structure is a feature of the world or socially constructed, our deconstructions are also constructed, and we neglect structure at our peril.

**JB:** Patrick Modiano's vicious 1968 satire *La Place de l'étoile* sketches, in brutally misogynist fashion, a critique of a post–World War II France trying to recuperate its republican and "terroirial" glory after the Nazi occupation. The text constantly shifts back and forth between Jewish assertiveness and an "adopted" Nazi pose, and between the time of Occupation and the time of writing, in the late 1960s. I read the book as an all-out attack on the idea that France's experience during World War II could be temporally quarantined in that fashion, and as an assertion, instead, that both that experience and the "recuperation" that followed it are of a piece with the chauvinist and imperialist aspects of French bourgeois republicanism.

Modiano's book centers on the person of his fictional hero and narrator, Schlemilovitch, and his fantasies of both aping and skewering the French bourgeoisie, blood-and-soil nationalists, homegrown antisemites, and Nazis, all in the time of narration, which is also the late 1960s. That was a time when it was possible to imagine that a liberal Europe was being reconstituted, and Modiano came to disrupt the notion that World War II and its genocide were aberrational vis-à-vis liberal Europe's vision of itself. Aside, as I mention, from the rank sexism from which the author seems to take no ironic distance, the difference between my reading of the book twenty-five years ago and now is that then, I focused on its examination of genocide within the heart of the metropole—thus, a spatial focus, whereas above (and here again), I am trying to focus on something like Modiano's representation of an extended nightmare (the narrative is ultimately presented as a nightmare described to Dr. Freud).

When I wrote *now* above I was not suggesting that I had anything radically new to think, nor was I proposing any particular recuperation, nor yet again any distinctive way in which this time is ontologically different from any time remembered or anticipated. It seems to me that I was trying to sneak up once again on what I might possibly mean by "a Jewish anthropology of the present." I am trying to get away from what seems the almost inevitable reflex of reflecting on the state of Jewish being as some point in a narrative arc from past to future. Notions of such an arc and the various forms it might take are crucial to many or perhaps most ideas of what "being Jewish" might mean; think of Gershom Scholem's distinction among conservative, restorative, and utopian moments in Jewish messianism.[3]

By contrast, I am trying to emphasize a now that is at once specifically Jewish—that is, a now that is filled with the extremely tenuous yet also enormously rich affect that a cultivated Jewish identity sustains in such obvious moments of danger—and at the same time fully bleeding into and suffused with the pathos of a moment that cannot count on any vision of a redeemed future to help get us through the night. Another way to say this: I want to consider the creative potential of articulating an ethical view that does not depend on expectation of future redemption, nor, indeed, on any assumed future whatsoever.

One of the risks of writing *now* is exemplified by your allusion to Gessen's writing. Your comments would (themselves) certainly fit very nicely into the *New Yorker*, as acid and literate commentary on the passions and fads of the day. And yet the present presses upon us and is not fully amenable to solace through irony or through the aspect of eternity; that is, as though it had already happened. I know I tend to take some comfort there, in the idea that the evil must take place because it will have taken place; and yet I stake the value of my critical stance on a skeptical attitude toward the slogan that "the arc of history bends toward justice."

In this respect, your comments on freedom are pertinent. In Timothy Snyder's little book *On Tyranny*, he urges us, among other things, not to be compliant before we are forced to.[4] I have perhaps become compliant far too soon. Is my colleague who still gets up at rallies and speaks about the necessary revolutionary alliance of the workers, the students, and the radical intellectuals doing better work?

But here's a last thought before I wish you, as we say on the Lower East Side, a *gutn shabbes*: a Jewish anthropology of the present would seek to draw out some of the particular Jewish resources for thinking about temporality that I alluded to above. This might in turn give clues to a possible sensibility (and perhaps eventually even forms of action) that would tend overmuch toward neither the fatalist complicity in which I often luxuriate nor the bravado of loudly asserted certainty of ultimate victory. An anthropology of the present, that is, focused on the particular awareness of mortality that has much to do with making us Anthropos, and that for centuries has driven Jewishness in some of its most creative directions.

**ML:** If I understand your reference to *La Place de l'étoile*, you sense in prominent attempts to repair the harms of the present moment a similar attempt to quarantine those harms as familiar deviation, offered within a worldview that asserts no cause for self-examination or radical reconstruction. In my mind, these attempts involve a certain unwillingness to recognize unpleasant relationships, and depend on a noncommittal awareness of causal necessity. I'll refrain from rearguing that case.

Parsing the phrase "a Jewish anthropology of the present," I understand "an anthropology" to mean a midrash that enlightens our notions of Anthropos using the tools that have been useful for anthropologists (a reflexive instance of anthropology's "man the toolmaker" narrative). I use the term *midrash* to avoid the language of description, accounting, or explanation that would return us to the problem of essence and teleology. A Jewish anthropology would presumably be an anthropology supplemented by various interpretive impulses that Jews recognize among ourselves and associate (by a particular interpretive impulse) with aspects of our shared experience. To focus on the present is to find something worth articulating now (which is to say, coincident with our invoking the word *now*). These articulations may appeal to teleological notions implicit in locating Anthropos and Jew, but should make no assumptions that firmly identify this asserted *now* with any specific point in a predetermined narrative arc. In particular, you wish to avoid the conclusion that, because circumstances lead us to describe the present moment (always existentially unique when we conjure it by name), this moment must be singular, corresponding to a defining inflection point in a plot embodying both *telos* and *logos*. Rather, this moment may just reflect the experience of things getting worse and worse along the way to continuing to get worse and worse, while we have already known much worse. If it once made sense to notice the spatial aspect of one or another nightmare, globalization has homogenized such distinctions (for people of a certain status in the first and second worlds). The texture of the nightmare now seems to vary largely in its temporal dimension, producing conditions that worsen over time within a familiar and largely static structure of geographical disparities.

As I understand Ruyer's *Neofinalism* (the fragments I have read), he sought to recover the possibility of judgment and purpose, protecting them from both teleology (comparison with some preconceived narrative) and social Darwinist anomie. In our context, suppose (just for the sake of argument) that over the next decade Moshiach does not come, but another world war does. Some might argue that while science can study the phenomena at hand, it cannot judge these events as success or failure. On this view, suffering is the obverse of the survival of others more fit, so that even if human evolution results in human extinction, well, that's just how it goes. Moreover, if science cannot judge this outcome to be a failure, then neither can philosophy or the humanities in general, because "we all know" that everything has a scientific explanation. But if we do judge this outcome a failure, it does not fully capture our judgment to assert disappointment that an alternative narrative in which we invested great faith did not emerge. We must admit that the collapse of a cherished messianic narrative would not be the most significant loss in the event of human extinction. To state the rather obvious (as Ruyer did), we judge such an outcome as a failure because it matters to us—to each of us subjectively and to all of us intersubjectively. For Ruyer (some years before our *Time and Human Language Now* [2008], but go know!) the scientific fact that unscientific subjective experience is known privately to each of us does not disqualify subjectivity, as some contemporary accounts of consciousness apparently aim to do. He argued that this knowledge points to that space where the humanities must proceed alone, leaving science behind because it can go no further. This view locates judgment precisely in that urge to offer a midrash to enlighten our notions of Anthropos.

We wish to articulate something valuable in the present about Anthropos and Jews, while preventing these essentialist notions from returning as argument-by-narrative, be it an ethnological present or a specifically Jewish fate. But we risk defying the insights of deconstruction when we posit Anthropos as distinguishable and coherent, let alone posit its consistent awareness of its presumed mortality. We struggle to avoid confusing signification with causality. Whatever account one might suggest for human mortality, we must avoid the fallacy that people die *because* they are mortal, or conversely that humans cannot cause our own extinction *because* we are merely human. Awareness of our mortality alludes to a generalization from multiple observations and a narrative conception for coping with it, but to say we are fated to die does not explain why we do, if that is something we wish to understand. In much the same way, finding something useful to say about the present depends less on locating ourselves within a teleological narrative than on our ability to focus on the material causality that assembles this ever-growing pile of wreckage into our now-persistent nightmare. Unfortunately, this focus leaves us staring blankly into a pair of inequivalent terrors: the utterly unknowable and the entirely predictable.

As we know, despite the foregoing pilpul (Talmudic argumentation) and an irritating popular characterization of narrative incoherence as "postmodern," contemporary failures of judgment are not expressions of a principled reluctance to impose preconceptions or a desire to maintain scientific objectivity. And as I've argued elsewhere, the crisis of judgment is better explained as disordered perception, a defense mechanism imposed by our minds to protect us from the excruciating experience of that nightmare from which we never awaken. In searching for something worth articulating at this particular present I find myself, by process of elimination, considering two possibilities. First, is there any means to effectively recommend Dr. Freud's response to a nightmare, which is to open one's eyes? Second, is there a possible replacement for current fashions in disordered perception (perhaps equally disordered) that might help pull us back from the abyss? As that growing pile of historical wreckage falls on us with greater speed, we must ask whether we can articulate, let alone know, what we mean by *Jewish* in this present? It goes without saying that posing the question to two Jews will elicit at least three different essentialist and teleological responses. But here in the very earthly city of Jerusalem, it seems increasingly obvious to a growing number of Jews that *Jewish* refers to an essentialist narrative of racial supremacy implying a teleology of power held not just by force of arms but also through imposed ideological conformity that rejects inquiry and critique as inherently foreign. Must we admit this as Jewish? We are now told (and school-children are educated to accept) that these new narratives are not a corruption of those that you and I have in mind when we speak of Jewishness. No, they were largely absent in our heritage because they have been hitherto "neglected," simmering quiescently because powerlessness cultivated a superficial patina of good-ness (and even many who object to such narratives are inclined to accept this explanation for their appear-ance). When my grandmother used to say, "A yid is in goless" (a Jew is in exile), I heard it as a statement of resignation—it never occurred to me that it could be an operational definition.

**JB:** It seems time to recur (once again). I have in a real sense nothing "new," usually a terror similar to that of the student faced with the blank page. You will recall more precisely than I the plaintive cry of a fellow student at Reed in the 1970s: "What can I say about Corot that hasn't been said already?" Any imagined reader of this admittedly somewhat hermetic text (let alone you,

Martin) has a right to expect it to move *forward*. Or as one might put it more viciously: Who are we to presume that our own words are worthy of seemingly endless commentary? Yet the strategy, or tack, of recurrence is I think quite apt here, on several grounds.

First, it seems consistent with Ruyer's articulation, as you summarize it, of a free act as one that sets out to exercise the human capacity of logic to see where it leads—as an act whose freedom is measured not by the novelty or the predictability of its achievement but by the coherence and autonomy of its moves. In that sense, even the brief exchange we have had so far within this document is susceptible to a "freedom check." And that recursive move—the suggestion that, already, we question what we have done here—suggests to me one point of access into what a Jewish anthropology might be. That point of access is, precisely, the culture of shared Talmud study, where somehow (this is not the place to defend what might seem to some a chauvinistic claim) it is possible to achieve an exhilarating degree of "open reading" of a text whose ultimate authority is fundamentally unquestioned according to the rules of the game of shared study. Precisely because the fundamental authority of the text is a given, both the worthwhile nature of this intense scrutiny and the ability of the text to bear such scrutiny without collapsing can be taken as givens. Therefore, the exhilaration comes from confidence that we can, in our limited freedom, push the text as hard as we want.[5]

The analogy to Talmud study leads me then to my second reason for asserting that recurrence is fitting here. Recurrence is what Talmud, as a process of study, does. It envelops, moves beyond and around, returns to, anticipates, never ends and never begins (every tractate famously begins with folio 2), at once already knows and has already contradicted itself. Talmud is ideally not goal-oriented. What is measured, I would say, is not the number of folios covered, nor even the "time spent" in study, but the amount of consciousness devoted to the text. In that respect, Talmud may be viewed as one of a vast (but not infinite, and arguably diminishing) number of models of genuine anthropological freedom, in Ruyer's sense. It is a key resource for a Jewish notion of anthropology; that is, the exercise of what still seem to be capacities quite distinctive to *Homo sapiens*, without necessarily implied teleologies or determinisms.

Third, recurring to our conversation as we have articulated it so far might enrich "now." By contrast, and here my recurrence begins, if I think of trying to say something wholly new, then I find myself faced, as you wrote above, with the terrifying choice between a "pair of inequivalent terrors—the utterly unknowable and the entirely predictable."

Not all that demands to be unpacked here will have that demand acceded to, not in the limited time left to us. (I keep thinking of a record of the great Polish Yiddish comic Shimon Dzigan, titled *Shimon Dzigan's Letster Gelekhter*; that is, his last laugh, which begins with him coming out on stage and asking the audience, "Vi shpet i' yetst"—that is, "How late is it?" It is not only the fact that this was his last recorded performance, but the fact that he spoke to an audience living in the shadow of the great *khurbn* (catastrophe), that immediately made me take him to be suggesting that limited time remained on a larger scale than that of one evening's performance.)

So let me say a bit more about at least two points mentioned above.

"The History of the Jewish Question as a Nightmare from Which We Will Never Awaken": I suggested this as an alternative title for our exchange here, but have done nothing so far to explain what resonance the phrase might have had for me when I first recorded it. It was indeed inspired directly by my rereading of Modiano, and by my perception of his brilliant and thoroughly unpleasant book as a commentary on the fatuousness of the notion that Europe after World War II had somehow awoken from the nightmare of fascism and, specifically, antisemitism. One might also read this takeoff on Joyce—his phrase, in *Ulysses*, is "history is a nightmare from which we are trying to awaken"—as a way to think about the self-understanding of at least some, if not all, varieties of Zionism: not as the culmination of Jewish history, not even as the Jewish "return" into history (in the famously Hegelian sense) but as an escape from the pathos of Jewish history into, I suppose, something like a Jewish spatial rather than temporal existence.

Yet I know that I wasn't, in fact, thinking of any critique of Zionism when I first recorded this phrase. We were then, in November 2017, closer in time to the Charlottesville horror of August 2017. Perhaps I can come closest to capturing my implicit understanding of the phrase then by saying this: Here I am, well aware that the Jewish question has never become obsolete, indeed that the poverty of discourse about what was once referred to as the Jewish question indicates not so much that it has been obviated or otherwise resolved, as the inadequacy of critical thinking "now" overall. Did

I really need history to come along and reassure me that my concerns were not only theoretical but entirely actual, that I might not have to work so hard in the academy (for example) as I did just a year or two ago to insist that Jewish difference remains a political issue? Did I really wish upon myself in some fashion, that is, such forceful confirmation that the "history of the Jewish question" remains an effective history? And might there be some way of escaping from that eternally recurring wash cycle by trying to articulate a present that is at once *Jewish* yet not dependent on a historical emplotment?

Here I draw on a specific, but brief, text from the Babylonian Talmud (Tractate Yevamos, folio 62a). In it some rabbis debate the minimal requirements for fulfillment of a commandment (understood here as only incumbent upon male Jews) to "be fruitful and multiply." According to Rav Huna, if a man had children but they died in his lifetime, he has fulfilled the commandment, but Rav Yochanan says that if his children die in his lifetime, he must have more children to replace the ones that have died. "Rav Huna said he has fulfilled the commandment based on Rav Assi's dictum: 'The son of David [Messiah] will not arrive until all the souls are vacated from *guf* [body].'" The authoritative twelfth-century commentator Rashi explains *guf* as a chamber containing all the souls created at Creation and waiting to be implanted into mortal bodies. Thus, according to Rav Huna, even a man whose children have died has done his part to find bodies for waiting souls and thereby advanced Messiah. Rav Yochanan cites, however, the verse that states that God created the world "to be inhabited"—and those who do not survive do not fulfill this requirement.

I find here a hint of a narrative arc that is not from "past" to "future." That is important to me, since I am not calling for a radical rejection of all possible forms of temporal articulations of meaning. This discussion in Yevamos suggests one possible avenue in a very old Jewish text toward a richer vocabulary of "authentically Jewish" temporalities. On one hand, Rav Huna's notion that the purpose of procreation is to see to it that all souls get their chance to become embodied suggests that mortal existence is not so much a collective effort to accomplish something as a process that must be endured; in that sense it is certainly eschatological but not especially teleological. On the other, Rav Yochanan's notion seems to have nothing to do with a Messianic end point, but to be entirely this-worldly and oriented toward the fulfillment of the work of Creation. One might therefore see this Talmudic text as offering an "existentialist" lesson that the life of Anthropos—another reading of *guf* here, though I don't have the source handy, is the body of *Adam Kadmon*, "Primordial Man"—is mandated to take place, and, I suppose, that if we extinguish ourselves before all of the souls in the *guf* have been embodied, then Messiah will never come.

All this may be taking us rather far from the current emergency, and in that sense from any conventional "now." Even so, we must remember to breathe; that is, to think. We tack back and forth. There is that which terrifies us, also you and I who continue to dwell in our relatively privileged and comfortable homes, who are still being paid, who are still insured, and for us (even more so for you, who expect so much from Anthropos, than for me) the terror is amplified by disappointment at the limited exercise of anthropological capacities. One thing that comforts us and helps us to breathe is the possibility of finding *khevrusa*, a camaraderie of exercise of anthropological capacity.

**ML:** Indeed, fear of the blank page may drive the tenured few to despair as readily as it inspires panic in students. To be fair, that plaintive cry (or perhaps, that plaintiff's cry) was about Shakespeare, not Corot, and so her bringing action against an expectation that she would say something interesting and original was perhaps a legitimate protest against an excessively high bar. But the blank page resting on the many millions of pages already piled up in the humanities continues to express a demand that we move *forward*, as you put it, if not temporally then at least in the consciousness we devote to the text that is now. We may find other grounds to leave a verdict of pointlessness unchallenged and sentence ourselves to silence—I'll return to that in a moment—but to confuse reexamination of previously accepted conclusions with unoriginality is misplaced in the humanities, as it is in the hard sciences (where teachers despair of incurious students who copy formulas from a book rather than engage with alternative approaches to puzzling questions about nature). The reasons you give for embracing recurrence elegantly refute the refutation of its value, an iterative refutation that, as Sergey Dolgopolski has written, characterizes the method of Talmud.[6] In this mode, I might reach your very conclusion by reversing the logic, and argue that in Talmud study, ultimate authority is fundamentally unquestioned precisely because it rests on the coherence and autonomy of the text, not merely on the reputation of its authors, and has been consistently found to withstand intense scrutiny without collapsing. (In the past, such a claim was also widely accepted for the authority of climate science.) Yet recurrence is also a source of vexation for my friends, who frequently challenge me to explain how "going over all this again," at ever more refined levels of articulation, can have an effect other than leading us into greater despair. Still, I remain stuck in the notion that some degree of freedom is to be found through the keen appreciation of (logical) necessity.

Your subtitle, "The History of the Jewish Question as a Nightmare from Which We Will Never Awaken," struck me as obvious, but in an admittedly nonobvious way. I remembered your phrase "the fatuousness of the notion that Europe after World War II had somehow awoken from the nightmare of fascism" while reading a review essay about the colonization of China from the Opium Wars to the Japanese occupation, when I learned that the author of the book under discussion "remains skeptical of the idea—characteristic of much contemporary Chinese scholarship—that the period amounted to an 'unrelenting Chinese nightmare.'"[7] In a Talmudic mode I wondered, what is the minimum level of hardship imposed by colonialism that renders the colonized permitted to feel that it is an unrelenting nightmare? This, in turn, reminded me of a verse from the TV police procedural *The Shield*, when an anticorruption investigator assures us, "Even the worst monster acts like a normal human being 80 percent of the time." So *pace* Stephen Dedalus, perhaps we should reserve some more literal term for the implicit 20 percent that is truly monstrous, and consider that the (always metaphorical) word *nightmare* may aptly designate the 80 percent of experience—under such circumstances—that is in some sense normal. After all, in its most basic definition a nightmare is a kind of dream, an experience that proceeds from mind to body, perhaps invoking bodily memory but not strictly dependent on real and present external conditions in the moment, and in principle it contains the possibility of restoration and repair by waking. Speaking of Dzigan: his last thirty-five years were spent in the shadow of the Catastrophe, not a mere nightmare from which one could fatuously imagine he could awake. At the time of his last recording, he had lived through multiple catastrophes in mid-century Eastern Europe, managing more than once to rebuild a life in the theater (complete with comfortable homes, salaries, and national health insurance), most famously with Israel Shumacher. And still, those last recordings were made in Israel, where the Yiddish language that was his life, along with its culture and humor, was often denigrated as symptomatic of a degenerated Jewish-history-as-nightmare, from which the state was determined to awaken us by force. This decline in fortune does not compare to the 20 percent catastrophe he knew in European prison camps, but may belong to the 80 percent nightmare of "normal" existence under this "return to history." I am reminded here of a Yiddish expression you taught me: G-d protect us from all the things we can learn to live with.

In the sense of this distinction, one can imagine that for some Europeans who speak of "what the Nazis did" while thinking of the relatively uneventful occupation of Bruges, fascism may indeed have been more of a nightmare than a catastrophe. It could also be said that for Jews (among others) born after 1945, World War

II was a catastrophe whose real historical consequences are still present in more ways than we imagine, but that also remains a nightmare, an unavoidable awareness that such a catastrophe did occur and hence continues to exist as a concrete possibility in the scheme of human affairs. As you say, theoretical concerns can become material with surprising rapidity and we should not require any new historical horrors to come along as motivation for enriching our grasp of theory. And yet, for so many at this moment, historical horror and catastrophe are materially present, and we may feel a strong countervailing impulse to "stop talking and do something." That impulse might even be persuasive if we knew what to do, which is to say, if we did not suffer all that poverty of discourse and inadequate critical thinking about so many things, including the Jewish question, whose failures of resolution now owe much to the efforts of certain Jews to preserve its historical misformulation and malformation. So here is the interface between nightmare and catastrophe—our nightmare prevents us from knowing how to effectively oppose catastrophe (even those catastrophes for which we bear some personal responsibility) and our inability to effectively oppose catastrophe feeds our nightmare.

A certain psychotherapist of my household responds to outbursts of the type "How could I have been so stupid?!?" by asking, "Are you asking that of yourself as a serious question?" If the Jewish question, as historically phrased, were actually a question rather than a set of somewhat misleading assertions constructed within an intellectual framework poorly suited to articulation of historical Jewish perspectives, it would probably still not be obsolete, but it might help the seemingly endless commentary move forward. Instead, it returns to confound our critical inquiry, much like a recurring nightmare, closing down the question rather than posing it seriously. Perhaps a more pertinent set of questions now would begin with, Why do categories and schemata within which Jews seem so anomalous persist as an ostensibly natural framework for sociopolitical discourse? Was it entirely necessary for Jews to accept an ill-fitting categorical agenda as price of entry to the Euro-American episteme, especially at Versailles after World War I? How did that agenda influence Zionist thought, especially the Hegelian "return to history," conceived as Hebrew-speaking assimilation into an imagined Europe (once known as gentile society) situated as a "villa in a jungle," claiming normality while reproducing existential foreignness and minority? How does the friction caused by traditional Jewish cultural impulses straining against ill-fitting definitions borrowed from Western sociology and politics affect life for Jews in Israel and Jewish relations with others? What inhibits a paradigm shift to a Jewish anthropology that would allow those impulses to appear natural instead of anomalous, and how would the Jewish question appear in such a frame of reference? Alas, pretty old questions. Does this move us forward?

For much of the world outside, Israel appears a beacon of neoliberal political economics powered by the familiar mix of science-based industry, kleptocratic oligarchy, and xenophobic "populism" that has metastasized in many developed societies. As elsewhere, opposition from the left to this state of affairs is generally deflected with pro forma textbook assertions about objectively correct economic relations and the impossibility of engaging with militant resistance to the state's self-conception. And when traditional Jewish concerns for justice, collective responsibility, defense of the weak, and the sanctity of life—even the lives of strangers—are raised, they are often acknowledged as honorable values that must nevertheless be balanced against limitations on what society can afford, limitations that somehow grow more severe as the country becomes wealthier and economic inequality reaches American levels. Thirty-some years ago, when prime minister Yitzhak Shamir cut the education budget in order to fund settlement building in the West Bank, he justified reducing the school day to just four hours by declaring that "a Jewish state has priorities." No longer construed as crass politicking, many view such thinking as making Israel great again. In its efforts to censor progressive NGOs and restrict their activities, the state promotes a narrative suggesting that Jewish values are not to be found in the biblical injunction to remember our history of oppression and refrain from oppressing others, but rather in a crude willingness to identify the state's critics with Pharaoh (if not Amalek). Words that once signified for me a Jewishness that was part of the way my particular soul inhabits the world are now used to define censorship of my own Jewish thoughts in the Jewish state. To be labeled a self-hating antisemite for protesting a catastrophe perpetrated by Jews in breach of Jewish tradition and values is not yet a distinct catastrophe, but it can reasonably be called a nightmare.

And I also find myself practicing a kind of self-censorship to avoid causing discomfort to the people

I care about. Especially since the American election of 2016, friends often ask me to avoid imagining out loud where things may be heading in the next decade or so. Certainly, if we are to have something worth saying about the present, we will first need to describe it critically. Reticence in judgment is a symptom of the nightmare from which we can't seem to awake. So many seem content to understand the present crisis as confined to the embarrassing drama of an unstable individual who cannot "act presidential" and the havoc he may unleash inadvertently. In this view, Trump breaks the fourth wall in the theater of hegemony, and if we can only dispatch this deviant, then the simulacrum of democracy, now intolerable in its operation, may be restored to normal functioning. This narrative, anticipating a restoration of natural order in 2020, focuses on the booming pronouncements of a certain great and powerful wizard, while admonishing us to pay no attention to those men behind the curtain turning the wheels and pulling the levers of power. Some do oppose this view, interpreting the crisis as the visible expression of a coherent political-economic program advanced by powerful interests, and not merely the frequently self-sabotaging machinations of a few public narcissists. But, perhaps reticent to judge, centrists often lump these progressives together with far-right conspiracy theorists as "populists," seeing a paranoid rejection of institutions as such, rather than sharp critique of particular institutional behavior. And while it may feel unreasonable that anyone could be intentionally directing the current insanity, with so much of the global system seemingly veering out of control, this apparent disorder may be symptomatic of a new and unfamiliar order as it appears from below.

You and I are now largely exempt from the worst material deprivations in class society. From the political revolutions of early modernity down to the postwar mixed economy, holders of real power acknowledged their interest in constructing this exemption. As John F. Kennedy (another billionaire president, of markedly different temperament) put it, "Those who make peaceful revolution impossible will make violent revolution inevitable."[8] Still, the concerted effort, begun in the 1970s, to reverse this trend is now widely recognized by its most familiar manifestation: globalization. This rollback, explicitly proclaimed in the Reagan-Thatcher era, was foreshadowed a few years earlier in the economic restructuring enacted in Israel by Menachem Begin under the guidance of Milton Friedman. Although Thatcher's famous claim that "there's no such thing as society" seems inconsistent with Jewish thought, Begin's privatization of resources that had been built over generations by organized labor and a nominally socialist state set the pattern for the later kleptocracies of post-Soviet Eastern Europe. The pattern is well known: accelerated globalization of business designed to disempower organized labor, disguise relations of ownership, and avoid taxation; the promotion of baroque theories in law and economics designed to reverse the postwar expansion of participation in democratic processes and impede government as a locus of collective activity; and most recently, the jamming of public communication channels through the intentional generation of noise mislabeled as information, including the substitution of simplistic pseudotheory for academic research. In parallel we are confronted with new defensive strategies that render the traditional tools of progressive politics—mass movements, organized protest, legal challenges, and moral leadership—increasingly ineffective, albeit not yet entirely so. Through these efforts the economic pyramid has come to resemble the ancien régime, with billionaires playing the role of an aristocracy wielding the exclusive power to influence the course of history, leaving everyone else scrambling to minimize immediate harm.

For many, the discourse of "economic inequality" refers to an ongoing catastrophe of poverty, and this must be distinguished from the nightmare of a middle class that (often repugnantly) experiences its own loss of position as far worse than catastrophe. Those called middle class are nonaristocrats (nonbillionaires) who nevertheless have sufficient economic and cultural resources to plan a trajectory through the capitalist landscape that steers between the Scylla of cultural deprivation and the Charybdis of sudden emergency (and so their access to rights guaranteed in law appears as a mark of privilege). We cannot endow a new hospital when we become ill, but do expect that health insurance (for those so lucky) will fend off the worst. The nightmare you and I share consists, then, in the dual consciousness of our inability to materially influence the present crisis and a foreboding that our exemption from its greater depredations may be temporary.

If government and business once (formally, at least) engaged in transparent and collaborative policymaking, we increasingly see powerful institutions managing their public presence in the style of information warfare, pursuing competitive advantage by manipulating public perception, for goals never made public. The chaos we see is often strategic opaqueness, the evasive dance of skilled con men (in Michael Bloomberg's apt phrase) feigning incompetence but quite effectively wielding government power for undemocratic aims.[9] This shift does enhance social mobility, but primarily downward mobility, as the characteristic privilege of the middle class—the capacity to make strategic decisions—becomes increasingly irrelevant for lack of access to reliable information. Between the nightmare of helplessness we feel in the face of catastrophic poverty and repression, and a nightmarish rollback that may aim to restore a pre-Enlightenment status quo, perhaps our greatest struggle now is resisting the impulse to turn away.

In this struggle, I concur (and recur) that Talmud as process is a good starting point, combining logic, insight, discipline, and the problems of everyday life. As you know, I can read "be fruitful and multiply" as two commandments, with the directive to multiply aimed primarily at those who have found some way to be fruitful. And so between the interpretation of Rav Huna and that of Rav Yochanan, I give greater weight to the latter, suggesting that souls (and other immaterial constructs such as ideas) must inhabit the world, over the former, suggesting that they must only be released from waiting. But the question is not entirely existential, because the stricter ruling of Rav Yochanan imposes an obligation, not just on the man whose children have died, but implicitly on the children he must bring as replacements. That's harsh. And without questioning Rashi, I would need to better understand his supposition that the number of souls created at Creation was finite. We have an obligation to bring new ideas into the world when old strategies lose their historical efficacy, just as *power* learns from our earlier successes and adapts. To inhabit this world is to be here together with what we are forced to confront at the moment, even if this seems a more daunting obligation than Rav Yochanan's. This is the freedom we find in Talmud study—to seriously question the validity of widely accepted conclusions without fear of causing the entire superstructure to collapse. Still, as Hasidim say, not everyone can live under such strenuous spiritual tension. I suppose that the problem of how strictly to impose that obligation, and upon whom, belongs to a Jewish anthropology of the present.

# 4

# On Being Always Already Unprepared for the Present

Gregory Starrett and Joyce Dalsheim

Marley was dead: to begin with. There is no doubt whatever about that. The register of his burial was signed by the clergyman, the clerk, the undertaker, and the chief mourner. Scrooge signed it: and Scrooge's name was good for anything he chose to put his hand to. Old Marley was as dead as a door-nail.

Mind! I don't mean to say that I know, of my own knowledge, what there is particularly dead about a door-nail. But the wisdom of our ancestors is in the simile; and my unhallowed hands shall not disturb it, or the Country's done for. You will therefore permit me to repeat, emphatically, that Marley was as dead as a door-nail. This must be distinctly understood, or nothing wonderful can come of the story I am going to relate.

—Charles Dickens, *A Christmas Carol*, 1843

*The Maharal of Prague, a Talmudic scholar who lived in the sixteenth century, distinguished between things that exist outside of time, such as the Torah, and ordinary human experiences, which occur "in time." Existing in time is the source of endless misery, because "every being in time is a being that has no rest, for time is dependent on motion that has no cessation ... and every being that is without rest is one of affliction."[1] In what follows, Gregory Starrett and Joyce Dalsheim discuss the quandary of living in time. This chapter is a slightly revised version of a dialog that took place at Cornell University in 2018.*

**Gregory Starrett (GS):** This book is called *The Jewish Question Again*, but it isn't really about Jews. If that astonishes you, dear reader, so much the better. Because that sense of astonishment, the sense of having been betrayed somehow, of knowing how things really are or ought to be and then being caught off guard by reality, is really the core of the matter. The question then becomes, Who, or what, is involved in that betrayal, as its perpetrator, its victim, and its subject?

**Joyce Dalsheim (JD):** Clearly, we are thinking with Walter Benjamin's observation about the trouble with astonishment at the current state of affairs.[2] Benjamin taught us that such astonishment reveals our mistaken ideas about history and temporality. But as we think about either surprise or betrayal, we might remember not only Dickens and Benjamin, but also Derrida invoking Hamlet's lament that "*The time is out of joint.* ... The age is off its hinges. Everything ... seems out of kilter, unjust, dis-adjusted. ... The world is going badly, the picture is bleak."[3]

**GS:** So, for whom is the age off its hinges? Prolific historian Joan Scott recently recalled her father's firing in the midst of the McCarthy era's anticommunist investigations:

> That was some sixty-five years ago. I thought all of it was long passed, a stage in my history—in American history—[that] we had all survived and that even some of its most ardent supporters had repudiated. So, I was unprepared for the power of my reaction to the election of Donald Trump: diffuse anxiety; a sense of fear in response to an indeterminate threat; dread about what would come next, as day after day more draconian measures were announced. It was, in some sense, the return of the repressed[,] and not only for me, but for the country as a whole.[4]

We will return to the "return of the repressed" and its Freudian heritage later. For now what is important is that Scott registered her emotional unpreparedness despite the focus of her own work. Or perhaps *because* of the focus of her own work. According to one of her professional websites, Scott has spent her career considering "the question of difference in history: its uses, enunciations, implementations, justifications, and transformations in the construction of social and political life."[5] After all that, she was nonetheless left unprepared for the present.

Intellectuals are afflicted by their idealism. We are hindered by the analytical categories and periodizations we work so hard to fashion, which become the stout chains and ledgers and money boxes we drag about like Jacob Marley, impediments to action that become visible to us only once it is too late to shed them. Despite understanding Derrida's spectral warning that the past is never closed, and Benjamin's stern admonition to abandon the notion of progress, we seem nevertheless to imagine that a better future is somehow always already promised to us. In Scott's case, the present has disrupted her sense that the misogyny and racism that structured the 2016 election—not to mention the ghostly Cold War politics of Russian geopolitical ambition—all these troubles, all these injustices, all these irrationalities should by all right and logic have been things of the past. Dead things, casualties of political, social, cultural, and moral progress. As utterly and completely dead as doornails.

**JD:** The disappointment and mourning at recent political events expose how even deep skepticism can succumb to the messages of modernity—its episteme, its categories, and its temporality. We deconstruct our own categories of humanity and our master narratives of progress as little more than social constructs. And yet, the more successful our critiques are as intellectual frameworks, the more disappointed we are when we have to live them. Despite our critiques, many of us still manage to envision a preferable future toward which we strive, and still believe in our human capacity to achieve. We might never come right out and say so, but our disappointment itself is telling. We could describe such a future with phrases like "the end of all forms of domination" or the achievement of "equal rights" or the enactment of "human rights," or simply the promise of democracy fulfilled, just as we imagine we can devise other ways of being in the world that would allow us to survive the current climate crisis.

In any case, the emancipatory promise of the future is one for which we know we must struggle, but also one we had convinced ourselves was already there for us to inherit. These constructs (equal rights, universal human rights), which are themselves tied to abstract bourgeois concepts of privilege, have the potential to glide right past the hard, immediate facts of racism and misogyny, of war and its devastation, displacement, statelessness, and starvation. (Think of Gaza or Yemen or Syria or Myanmar now, or of the Indian census in Assam that threatens to decertify millions of people as Indian citizens and push them across the border into Bangladesh.) We often attend to these as separate problems, each one a case unto itself—as if misogyny, racism, xenophobia, and state-lessness were all separate issues; as if all these troubles could be disentangled from climate change. Despite all our theorizing, we have yet to fully grasp our own complicity in the structures of inequality and violence, or to integrate such an understanding into our actions and our lives, which leaves us once again astonished. This hearkens back to the voice of Koheleth, the sage who speaks in Ecclesiastes, quoted at the open-ing of this book. Koheleth speaks about the human inability to fully make sense of the world, and how this frustrates us again and again. It's a fundamental frustration with being human. We know "we are only human" but continuously struggle to come to terms with our limitations.

**GS:** And the universality of those limitations always takes a thousand local forms. The 2016 elections in the United States, and all the other sharp turns to authoritarian nationalism that happened around the world—in addition to India, think Brexit, Hungary, Poland, Brazil, the Philippines—were merely an institutional confirmation of other crises. We already knew that in the United States black men and women were being murdered by police or neglected in custody to the point of death with seeming impunity, triggering an international movement reminding us that Black Lives Matter. Seemingly overnight, Confederate statues and memorials across the United States sprang to life again, summoning popular movements to dismember and inter them, to place them in protective custody, or otherwise to settle on what they meant. Immigrants are rounded up and incarcerated by special squads of federal police who forcibly separate parents from their children as preludes to deportation. We knew that xenophobia against immigrants and refugees, and hate crimes against Muslim and other minorities, had been on the rise. But then attention shifted to the well-known secret that powerful men prey sexually on the women with whom they work and the children who have been entrusted to their care. And then it shifted again, to images of refugees who have drowned as they seek asylum in the West, and then back to those migrants on the US-Mexico border placed in cages without legal recourse, without clean water or medical care. We argue about whether such facilities deserve to be called concentration camps. "Where a chain of events appears before us" (**JD:** or perhaps a tangled series of exceptional incidents we take to be more or less unconnected to one another), Benjamin's angel of history sees a single catastrophe. Our astonishment leads us to imagine we've moved backward along the tracks, rather than to focus our vision on the pile of historical wreckage, "what we call progress," mounting to the sky.

**JD:** And yet this temporality reemerges, looking toward the elections of 2020 in the US: we can still move forward, it's not too late, we just need to get back on track.

**GS:** The Syrian uprising, the war against the Islamic State, and other political crises have created the largest population dislocations since the Second World War, providing new images of sprawling refugee camps and homeless families turned away at state borders or drowned when their overcrowded boats capsize, reminding us of the scratchy newsreels of the 1930s and 1940s. Its own homeland now secured as a result of those harrowing journeys of the past, Israeli predation of the scattered and dwindling land still possessed by Palestinians continues with the increasing support of enthusiastic American Christians—colonialism persisting into the postmodern present. All of these return to our consciousness as vicious and shocking anachronisms. (**JD:** The time is out of joint.) But perhaps even more shocking than the events themselves is the loss of confidence that we can speak about them properly, that we can find reliable theories or methods of analysis, or maintain public respect for the cosmopolitan ideas of social progress.

**JD:** Now you've lost me, really. Who is the "we" here? What cosmopolitan ideas? Because, in a very real sense, "we" scholars have been critical all along of believing in such progress, and of the problems inherent to modernity—think of Adorno and Horkheimer ...

**GS:** Perhaps, but not all "we scholars" are created equal. Adorno and Horkheimer never pulled the levers of real power. I'll meet your Adorno and raise you Woodrow Wilson, Paul Wolfowitz, Lawrence Summers, and the whole *New York Times* financial/military/journalistic complex.

**JD:** Out damn spot! Out, I say!

**GS:** One of the reasons "modernity" has a chance is that its critics, in the name of understanding it, have reified and reproduced it by pretending that critical consciousness itself is a form of transcendence.

**JD:** And now we hear formerly radical voices calling for a *return* to the liberal order, defending what they once critiqued because this move away from the liberal order seems to be pushing us "backward" rather than forward toward increasing social justice. And realizing that this is happening—that, too, is astonishing! Maybe even more astonishing and disempowering than the illiberal present.

**GS:** Perhaps this is because critiques of liberal modernity are themselves so internally complex and contradictory. In some ways that liberal order has been most cogently described not by John Locke or John Rawls, but by Marx and Engels in the opening pages of the *Communist Manifesto*:

The bourgeoisie ... has put an end to all feudal, patri-archal, idyllic relations. It has pitilessly torn asunder the motley feudal ties that bound man to his "natural superiors" and has left remaining no other nexus between man and man than naked self-interest ... It has drowned the most heavenly ecstasies of religious fervor ... in the icy water of egotistical calculation. It has resolved personal worth into exchange value, and in place of the numberless indefeasible chartered freedoms, has set up that single, unconscionable free-dom—Free Trade. ...

... All fixed, fast-frozen relations, with their train of ancient and venerable prejudices and opinions, are swept away, all new-formed ones become antiquated before they can ossify. All that is solid melts into air, ... and man is at last compelled to face ... his real conditions of life, and his relations with his kind.

The need of a constantly expanding market ... chases the bourgeoisie over the whole surface of the globe. It must nestle everywhere, settle every-where, establish connexions everywhere.

... In place of the old local and national seclusion and self-sufficiency, we have intercourse in every direction, universal inter-dependence of nations. ... National one-sidedness and narrow-mindedness become more and more impossible, and from the numerous national and local literatures, there arises a world literature.

... In one word, [the bourgeoisie] creates a world after its own image.[6]

In this brutal but elegant vision of transformation one might find an explanation for the remaining outbreaks of religious or ethnic or national conflict. Capitalism was supposed to have replaced local and premodern hierarchies with a new form of oppressive interchangeability.

**JD:** That is, if we insist on understanding social reality as always necessarily moving forward toward something better, then ...

**GS:** Then these must be reactionary forces, the last spasms of outmoded structures of domination struggling for life against capitalism's universal leveling of difference to mere exchange value. But we don't like either of those alternatives. We want cosmopolitanism to be possible without alienation, and equality to be possible as something other than equivalence.

**JD:** Or, if we insist on progressive temporality, then it is Gramsci's "morbid symptoms" that appear in the interregnum, when the old is dying but the new has yet to be born.[7] But this time, we sense that "new" is nowhere on the horizon, and instead we have switched directions.

**GS:** In Charlottesville, Virginia, in 2017, rallying neo-Nazis and Klansmen chanted, "You will not replace us! Jews will not replace us!" Since then the pile of wreckage has continued to grow, as Muslims are murdered at prayer in Christchurch, New Zealand, because they are imagined as invaders intent on replacing white people, or Jews slaughtered at prayer in Pittsburgh because they are imagined to be encouraging migrants from Central America to massacre white Americans, or Latinos gunned down in an El Paso Walmart because they threaten to use up all "our" natural resources. This rhetoric is traced to French writer Renaud Camus, who has proposed a "great replacement" theory, in which immigrants are swamping the civilized West. In tones that echo Marx's contempt for the reduction of human value to cash exchange,

> Camus derides [French president Emanuel] Macron, a former banker, ... as someone who thinks of people as "interchangeable" units within a larger social whole. "This is a very low conception of what being human is," [Camus] said. "People are not just things. They come with their history, their culture, their language, with their looks, with their preferences." [Camus] sees immigration as one aspect of a nefarious global process that renders obsolete everything from cuisine to landscapes. "The very essence of modernity is the fact that everything—and really everything—can be replaced by something else, which is absolutely monstrous."[8]

This diagnosis, like Marx's, blames capitalism for our current problems. Some contemporary racists want to emphasize difference because of their horror of a denatured human being devoid of any qualities but exchange value. An abstract human being forged by the same kind of corrupted modernity about which Adorno and Horkheimer wrote. But what, then, has happened to our understanding of the difference between the critiques of a Marxian Left and the critiques of a resurgent Right? We've both written, elsewhere, about the fragility of social theory. You've pointed out that activist preference for praxis, and even for justice, prevents us from applying certain elements of critical theory—regarding identity, for example—in a consistent way.[9] I've argued that formal social theory has so permeated our lived experience that we can no longer use it to illuminate the social structures it has inspired.[10] Here, Camus plays with the idea of culture and the dignity of peoples in ways that remind us of how white South Africans deployed an ideology of "culture" to prop up apartheid.

**JD:** And so, by this analysis, racism is a "backlash." It is a thing of the past that returns to rail against the forces of cosmopolitan modernity. What's missing, of course, is what Marx didn't quite grasp, that modern capitalism emerged not in the homogenization of global bourgeois culture, but in the brutal structural division of the world into categories of slavers and enslaved. Racism both enabled and emerged from exploitation. It is baked into the modern world system. Racialization cannot be reduced to class distinctions. Indeed, recently we have heard scholars describe the ways in which modern categorizations of race, ethnicity, nation, and religion are expressions of modernity, which scholars like Webb Keane—failing to acknowledge their debt to Jonathan Boyarin—have described as the "Christian modern."[11]

**GS:** Keane's finely focused historical ethnography of Dutch colonialism in Indonesia has bled, unfortunately, into yet another grand temporal scheme. The whole point of thinking in terms of the "Jewish question" is that these theoretical distinctions are ideological ones with deeper roots than Keane's imaginary Calvinism of "the modern." They emerge from ancient discussions of the difference between pagans and Jews, and the place of the Jews in the new dispensation of Christianity, and then in the very Catholic blood-purity laws of Iberia and its colonies in the New World, as Irene Silverblatt has shown.[12] But even thinking in terms of "modernity," Christian or otherwise, turns us back (**JD:** And now you're arguing implicitly that *theory* is progressive!), hopelessly, into the very categories of difference, progress, periodization, and linearity we're trying to question.

**JD:** Indeed, modern debates about emancipation have been formulated precisely around such categories as "ethnicity" and "religion," which presume these aspects of identity to be divisible, discrete, and mutable attributes of individual identity.[13] But theories of race also marked some people—including Jews—as immutably such, regardless of the separate category of religion and regardless of individual practices. All of which might suggest that dismantling racism also entails *dismantling its foundational Christian modern episteme.*

**GS:** Enough with the "modern" already! What keeps us using such a periodization apart from a vain insistence on our own uniqueness?

**JD:** OK, OK, I get it! We'll never understand what's going on unless we can imagine continuities with much longer historical processes. Our problems are not modern; they are linked to Pope Innocent IV, you say. And Jonathan Boyarin tells us we have to think back to Eusebius—whoever that is!

Perhaps more to the point, we must consider Walter Benjamin's thinking about history, historicism, and historical materialism. True historical materialism should conceive of history in ways that serve the struggle of the oppressed. A certain theology was required "to re-establish the explosive, messianic, revolutionary force of historical materialism."[14] Benjamin thought that historical materialism should not, in fact, accept the idea of necessary stages of progress. Instead, he suggested an alternative conception that breaks open what seems to be the natural progress of history by way of a "tiger's leap" into the past that can blast apart that continuum. This means that interpreting historical materialism as the idea that racism is just backward or a backlash against progress is a misunderstanding of the liberatory potential of historical materialism.

GS: We're confusing levels of analysis here: to say that "racism is backward" is a description of the lived reality of those who are astonished about Charlottesville and Pittsburgh and Christchurch, not of the idealized liberatory potential of either theory or revolution. It's the illusory temporality underlying that lived reality that we're trying to understand.

JD: Those levels are not so easily separated! But, since you have raised the idea of "abstract human beings" in order to provoke me, Hannah Arendt's point was precisely that the "'abstract' human being" is an *idea*.[15] It might be one that pleases the liberal imagination, but in reality it exists nowhere. In reality there are groups of more and less powerful people who organize themselves and look after those they count as among their own. She suggested that the idea of universal human rights was based on that idea—an idea that many of us would promote, but that becomes meaningless. This idea of universal humanity might be precisely what drives the fearful imaginings that lead to opposition to immigration, such that potentially liberatory universal humanism entails its own rejection. The fear of replacement might rely on a notion of abstraction in the sense that one human can replace another in a particular job, for example. And Arendt, again, would warn us that while one person might work for lower wages than another, that exchange does not guarantee civil and human rights to the migrant. Quite the opposite, in fact! But your Camus …

**GS:** *My* Camus??

**JD:** Yes, *your* Camus—he's not talking about abstract human beings replacing one another because all humans are of equal value and should be afforded equal rights. Instead he talks about a kind of reverse colonization, by which black and brown people pose a demographic threat to white Europeans, which we might as easily read as Christian Europe for all that both of those designate an unmarked category.

This is all about identity, all about the thing called "Europe" about which Susan Buck-Morss asks: "Does such a thing as Europe exist that is threatened by the future, or is the future [a] threat to the concept, Europe, itself? Does Europe have any existence other than as a signifier? Is it an idea, or a place? Does it mean shared cultural values like democracy, tolerance, and liberty, or shared cultural identity embodied in only certain kinds of Europeans? Precisely what, or who is that Europe, the future of which is under threat?"[16] She wrote this in response to a conversation about antisemitism and Islamophobia in Europe—which continue to play out in the fears stoked by this Camus and his replacement theory.

This book, we said, is not really about Jews—but then again, it is. It is about the Jews "as a kind of originary and constitutional alterity, or otherness," as Cynthia Baker explains, "the alpha to the Christian omega; the 'Old' to the Christian 'New'; the 'particular' to the Christian 'universal.'"[17] The idea of "the Jew" serves as a marker of that which "we" (white, male, European, Christians) are not. Thinking time as progress in which the new replaces and improves upon what came before is thinking in Christian terms.

**GS:** No. This merely substitutes the grand category of "Christianity" for that of "modernity" as the source of an ideology of progress. Are we discussing formal theology, or cultural practices, or a critical appraisal of either one?

**JD:** Those white supremacists who chant, "the Jews will not replace us," are thinking in precisely such terms. Christianity must triumph, otherwise progress is being undermined, things are going backward. Those among us who experienced shock at the outcomes of the 2016 US presidential election share a temporal imaginary with those white, Christian supremacists, even as we fill that imaginary with different desires.

The historical Jewish question has been transformed in multiple ways. In Europe, the Syrian refugee now takes the place of "the Jew." And in the Middle East, we may say, with Ilan Halevi, that the immigration of several hundred thousand European Jews into

Palestine and its accompanying expulsion of several hundred thousand Palestinians "introduced the 'Jewish question,' hitherto essentially a European question, into the heart of the tragedy of the Arab people of Palestine," where there then "arose the 'Palestinian question.'"[18] But for the Jews themselves, the Jewish question did not end with the establishment of the modern state of Israel. It was simply transformed there.[19]

**GS:** Transformed. *Replaced.* Joan Scott explained her shock and unpreparedness as a passive reaction to an actively unreasonable present, the "return of the repressed," a kind of haunting by what should have been dead and gone. Freud wondered about why our memories fail to reflect our experience. How can our descriptions of what has happened to us, and our *explanations* for how we have become what we are, not only be wrong, but actively conceal the truth? He answered that we may actually have no memories *from* the past, but only memories *relating to* the past, showing us not what the past was like, but how it *seems* to have been, how we might like it to have been, at the time those memories are aroused. These "screen memories" protect us from truths we would rather not acknowledge. If our understanding of the past is primarily about protecting ourselves from it, about making sure the past stays there and doesn't bother us now (**JD:** So that the time will not be out of joint.), then what does our current astonishment mean?

Our perceptions of how we got here are screens in a double sense. They are both barriers that block our view of what has gone before and surfaces onto which we project a preferable alternative, a desired past that comfortably explains familiar joys and suffering, even if that desire is perhaps for the past to have been something truly horrible, by comparison with which the present is a step forward. A sign that an even better future might be possible. What appears to be a broad collective reappearance of such a horrible past, now, like Jacob Marley's restless ghost climbing noisily out of the cellar, not only shocks us and leaves us feeling unprepared, but presents several other problems. (**JD:** Except, of course, for those people who voted for this and who are likely to understand this present precisely as indicative of progress.)

Such reappearance disturbs the metaphors that represent the wisdom of our ancestors, without which, according to Dickens's narrator, "The Country's done for." The sense that progress is inevitable and that things will get better is a profound hope. But it dooms us not only to intellectual error but to active complicity. Jacob Marley laments that the dead are tormented by their inability to affect the world. The duty of each person in life is to extend one's spirit to others and relieve their suffering. Death emphasizes the knowledge of this duty without the means to effect it, dooming them to misery as perpetual, helpless witnesses of suffering's eternal present. The living who fail to understand this are "captive, bound, and double-ironed," able but unwilling to confront injustice during life. Like the chained spirits who are newly willing but unable, they, too, are useless, as dead as doornails.

**JD:** "One reason why Fascism has a chance," Benjamin told us, "is that in the name of progress its opponents treat it as a historical norm."[20] And so, we ask of our current astonishment: With what does such a reaction make us complicit now? Framing the present as the unexpected recapitulation of a rejected or ignored past reminds us of who the "we" is in Scott's "we had all survived." It rests on the discourses of a public sphere in which racial and gender prejudice—and even class stratification and focused political persecution—might comfortably be ignored since they do not represent the lived realities of anyone who really matters. Having been caught unprepared for the present is a symptom of social position. Which leads me to ask: *Who* was astonished and by what? Who was not astonished at all? What can these differences teach us about social theory, power relations, positionality, and temporality?

**GS:** According to Derrida, what seems to be the return of the past as specter reminds us of other ancestors, other histories and inheritances, and other ways of placing ourselves relative to *an unclosed past* that has never disappeared. Derrida's view of spectrality denies the distinction between past and present, while that of Dickens denies the distinction between present and future. The only hope in either case lies in the knowledge that comes from lifting the screen separating now from not-now. For Benjamin, the openness of the not-now we think of as past calls for an interchange in which its meanings and its very nature must be achieved in the present. "The past can be seized only as an image which flashes up at the instant when it can be recognized and is never seen again. ... For every image of the past that is not recognized by the present as one of its own concerns threatens to disappear irretrievably."[21]

**JD:** "The current amazement that the things we are experiencing are 'still' possible in the twentieth century is *not* philosophical," Benjamin continued. "This amazement is not the beginning of knowledge—unless it is the knowledge that the view of history which gives rise to it must be abandoned [*nicht zu halten ist*]."²² If we understand the problems that arise from this view of history, including the dilemma of being constantly surprised that the present is not what it ought to be, and that therefore we are unprepared to live in it, what other ways of conceptualizing the past are available for us to think and act with?

What might it mean to think, for example, "in Jewish"?—with a nod, again, to Jonathan Boyarin, who wrote a book with that title.²³ How might we conceive an alternative temporality emphasizing the recurrence or repetition of experience without falling into the trap of "Amalek," of presuming that hatred of Jews—or Muslims, or strangers and migrants—is eternal regardless of the specific historical context? And what would it mean to think with Benjamin in terms of "dialectical images" that can disrupt history because the concept of progress is demobilizing, and to take seriously his insistence that nothing can be accomplished without also rescuing the dead? Every year at the Passover seder, we ask what it means to really remember your ancestors, by identifying with their struggles and seeing yourself "as if you had yourself been freed from slavery in Egypt,"²⁴ which suggests a very different way of being in time than most of us are used to. We might ask ourselves what it would mean to really remember the French Revolution, or May Day, or the civil rights struggle. What would it mean to think with Max Weinreich in terms of panchronicity, in which nothing is necessarily out of time, and there are no anachronisms?[25] Or with Derrida in terms of haunting specters? For me, really, this idea of living as though "you too had been brought forth from Egypt"—that really is the challenge …

# 5
# Responses (the Jew, the Muslim)

Gil Anidjar

Whatever accounts for the perdurance of the state of affairs in Israel/Palestine, it clearly has planetary dimensions. Accordingly, any understanding of the "Jewish question" and the "Muslim question,"—an understanding so likely to begin and end (albeit for understandable reasons) in the eastern Mediterranean— must resist confinement to this most manifest site, precisely because of the interminable, local urgency. So much for the geography lesson. But even a fragmented historical sense would have to acknowledge that the present is hardly exhausted by its harsh novelty or by its walled locality. Nor is the popular construction of a "past" Jewish question that would have been replaced by a current Muslim question tenable. Entanglements, avoided with little regard for their unavoidability, are thicker and more complex as they extend into the past, a past that continues to be in need of understanding and reframing. Indeed, for those who, otherwise up to date on the historical front, would trace this specific instance of modern hostility back to the early chapters of settler colonialism (but how many promised lands are we prepared to count?), there are others with a different memory who foreground two World Wars (Sykes-Picot, the United Nations) as well as the Holocaust (the Jewish question), not to mention Orientalism and Islamophobia, or might go back to the Crusades (Jerusalem!), in the creation of the brutal and unstable status quo. The dismantling of the Ottoman Empire will perhaps one day register as having given us our longest century yet. On the hither side of history (finally?), the uncertain end of the Cold War has made China and India (along with "older" players like Europe—including Russia—and the United States) increasingly potent and pertinent actors—remarkably anti-Islamic actors all, in effect if not in intent. And then there is oil, gas, and water, the security/securities complex (finance, arms production and trade, technology at large), the growth of nuclear plants and arsenals, real or imagined, and still, Israelis and Palestinians, Jews and Arabs, Muslims and Jews, as well as Christians, too ("United for Israel," and not) of every origin and denomination.

The planetary dimensions, the planetary constitution, of every problem plaguing our imagination and the rest of our existence only underscore, however, the remarkable similarities we undoubtedly witness here and elsewhere (walled states and walled selves). From capitalism to populism, from migration, Islamophobia, and religion to "the environment" (abbreviated euphemisms all for interacting and intra-acting entanglements, as Karen Barad has it, finding inspiration in the work of famed nuclear scientist Niels Bohr[1]), our tired gazes move screenways to the local and to the global, from nationalist echo chamber to economic and digital bubbles with cyber and other defenses on the alert. So why still, why again and why especially, the Jew, the Arab?

In the following, I wish to revisit an answer I tried to substantiate in *The Jew, the Arab: A History of the Enemy*.[2] Here, I want to continue exploring the way the Jew, the Muslim (I register, as I did in that book, the semantic oscillations that mark and affect these names) constitutes a persistent *form* of our multifarious entanglements. Its significance as "the enemy's two bodies," an inextricable and organizing theologico-political nexus, functions as the manifest and sedimented frame of a complex and enduring history (figured perhaps most manifestly, I argued, in those two Shakespearean characters on the cusp of modernity, Shylock and Othello, race and religion) and as an artificial diversion inscribing exceptional and protracted impossibilities, inhibiting understanding and preventing transformations other than ossifications. Why diversion? Growing immiseration, the weaponization of every GPS'd artifact perfected toward surveillance and tracking, management and control, or "targeted" killing and bombing, with advances often developed and tested by the Israeli military complex ("Unit 8200" and ubiquitous drones, among other instances, having gained relative visibility) or by Google and Facebook with a little help from diverse, or the same, frenemies (US and European foreign policy, immigration, Islamophobia) along with ever more apparent environmental devastation (the Great Pacific Garbage Patch and radioactive isotopes have invaded, like proliferating floods, every living being, it seems)—these challenges on our deficient attention can surely comfort us in the conviction that we have all become "better angels of our nature" or, more plausibly, I think, force us to acknowledge that violence is not the exclusive measure of our ongoing destruction.

I shall be guided by a singular piece of writing, recently translated into English, which strikingly stages the inextricability of the Jew, the Arab, of the Jewish question and the Muslim question, and does so in a truly thought-provoking manner. In *Whites, Jews, and Us: Toward a Politics of Revolutionary Love*, Houria Bouteldja recasts a long history that layers the present moment, while offering numerous glimpses, at times refreshing vistas, toward a radical transformation of— at the very least an invitation for resignification with regard to—these "questions," their historical separation, and more.[3]

# Responses

Writing in the wake of the dissolution of identities—and their simultaneous hardening—Bouteldja addresses the Jews (not only the Jews, obviously, but it is the chapter of her book where she does so that will guide me here). The chapter—indeed, the entire book—constitutes an open letter, a series of direct, audacious, and controversial interpellations, distinct from the "dialogues" that, elsewhere in the public sphere, have more often taken the form of irenic exchanges, calls to peace and understanding, as if the matter were one of mere goodwill (granting that that, too, is of course lacking). Inspired by Frantz Fanon and others, Bouteldja writes in a different voice, in a distinctive and challenging tone, and leaves little off the table. She writes in French and in France, from a divided and expansive France, yet she insists on adopting and deploying a global and oppositional perspective, very much within the rift that separates, or seems to separate, the Jew from the Arab, the Jewish from the Muslim question. Although she embraces a specific set of explicit coordinates for the conversation she initiates and carries, Bouteldja is careful to acknowledge other, no less explicit, elements that link the two questions: the events and the trajectories that bind her to her addressees. Within a quick few lines, she manages to evoke Israel, the Holocaust, colonialism, Sephardic (or Arab) Jews, and the familiarity as well as the hatred that undoubtedly exists between Jews and Arabs. She goes on to recall a shared belonging to the "religions of the book" and a common Abrahamic genealogy. But Bouteldja seeks a different kind of kinship (she recalls the familiar and familial trope of "cousins"), a political kinship in the colonial aftermath. And she locates this kinship in the fraught relation to whiteness, in the relation of and to the Christian and colonizing West (with which she engages in a previous chapter). According to Bouteldja, Jews—by which she means the public, often institutional voices that, multifarious and diverse, yes, nevertheless make vocal claims as Jews and for Jews, for and about the "Jewish state" and the Jewish people, from Israeli politicians to Jewish organizations, leaders, and "lobbies," to other, rarely elected, public figures, intellectuals, rabbis, and so on—have overwhelmingly entrenched themselves, have defined and defended their position, within the theologico-political arrangement and geopolitical borders of the West. Embracing the slow and ambiguous promises of their "emancipation"—often enacted in the shape of state and colonial decrees—Jews have come to embrace and incarnate the most essential aspects of modernity (Yuri Slezkine, for his part, restricted his proximate claim to "capitalism, communism, and nationalism" in his account of "the Jewish century"[4]). Finding an ambiguous resource in Sartre, Bouteldja sees the Jews for what they have become, for their proximity to and alliance with the Christian West in the modern dispensation.

Bouteldja does not spare harsh and difficult words. She insists on the conflicts, the struggles—the betrayals, the lies, the deception, not to speak of the genocidal violence—that are involved in what has passed for emancipation, the more or less willing integration of the Jews into the West (and think of the current laments over the lack of integration of Muslims), the embrace of France (but she could have

said: of Britain, of Germany, or of the United States;
she could have said of Christianity, and she indeed
points to the Christian West at large), the enthusiastic
acceptance of philosemitism. Bouteldja recognizes,
but also questions (as many Jews themselves question), the multifarious and often contradictory ideological choices that have been made by Jews, as well
as for and about Jews, choices that gain from being
acknowledged as they structure the public presence
of Jews in political and cultural discourse, determining as well the limits of tolerable speech ("Today the
notion that Human Rights Discourse is still about
the Jews takes the form of a taboo against saying so,"
writes Robert Meister, as he asks "Still the Jewish
Question?"[5]). It is true, Bouteldja says to the Jews,
"You were really chosen by the West. For three cardi-
nal missions: to solve the white world's moral legit-
imacy crisis, which resulted from the Nazi genocide,
to outsource republican racism, and finally to be the
weaponized wing of Western imperialism in the Arab
world" (55). This "deal with the devil" has wrought
a massive transformation, one for which Bouteldja
spares, I have already said, no harsh words. Jews have
come to love the white, Christian world. They have
allied themselves with it, accepting its ambiguous
protection. In striking turns of phrase that evoke the
status of Jews (and other minorities) under Islamic law
as well as the (French) colonial policies that, dividing
and ruling, mobilized and weaponized "favored"
colonized minorities against colonized populations,
Bouteldja avers that "in the span of fifty years, you
went from being pariahs to being, on the one hand,
*dhimmis of the Republic* to satisfy the internal needs of

the nation state, and on the other, *Senegalese riflemen* to satisfy the needs of Western imperialism" (56).

With a phrase that brings together evocatively, and with a heavy dose of historical irony, the divisions and rules of race and religion, of religion and politics, of colonialism and anti-Semitism, Bouteldja intends to jar and shock, but the shock is meant to provoke recognition. She seeks to ignite knowledge anew and to unsettle, to remind us of the long history that has separated Arab from Jew, Judaism from Islam, in a complex and discontinuous trajectory, which has deep roots in the Christian theologico-political imagination, in textual sources and in institutions that accompany and even govern the Christian West since its medieval inception and through its colonial ventures. At the tail end of this history, to which the colonized, the migrants, and the Muslims are equal (and, of course, unequal) heirs—it is only to the Jews, for instance, that Spain has recently offered an uncanny "right of return" for 1492—Bouteldja calls on the Jews to acknowledge the price of their success: "You have abandoned the 'universalist' struggle by accepting the Republic's racial pact: white people on top, as the legitimate body of the nation, us as pariahs at the bottom, and you, as buffer. But in an uncertain, uncomfortable, in-between" (56). The hierarchy is clear, as is the uncertainty—the permanent worry and much-clamored vigilance with regard to anti-Semitism—that is generated by the position Jews have come to occupy in relation to whites and to the colonized masses. And recall that the perspective Bouteldja adopts is, once again, global. She foregrounds France (where she lives) and Israel, but the import of her words is unmistakable in its reach.

From now on, you are stakeholders in the "Judeo-Christian civilization." Admit it. It's sad that this rehabilitation has been conditioned by genocide, by your partial self-expulsion from Europe and the Arab world for Israel, and by your renunciation to fully reclaim a France which is, nevertheless, yours. ... Two birds one stone: they got rid of you as pretenders to the nation and as historical revolutionaries, and made you into the most passionate defenders of the empire on Arab soil. ... They managed to make you trade your religion, your history, and your memories for a colonial ideology. You abandoned your Jewish, multi-secular identities; you despise Yiddish and Arabic and have entirely given yourselves over to the Zionist identity. In only fifty years. (57)

The ambiguous successes of the alleged resolution of—rather than a responsible response to—the Jewish question are here piercingly highlighted, and so consistently from a dual perspective: Jewish and Arab, Jewish and Muslim. The costs, the losses, are acknowledged from within a clear and politically committed interpretive position, from a deep empathy for loss (of language, of tradition, of history, and of communal alliances; of conflict, too) and with a sense of shared, if obviously unequal, fate. Bouteldja lingers with—she probes at—the worry and the doubt that define the Jewish political sense, as expressed through countless public and official assertions regarding Israel, anti-Semitism, and the all-too-eager celebrations of "Judeo-Christian civilization."

Another cost Bouteldja acknowledges is, of course, the growing distance and the contagion of hatred, which further efface possibilities of solidarity and cements, for the Jews, the choice of the Christian West—the historically anti-Semitic West!—over an Arab or Muslim past and present; which further cements, that is, the place the Jews occupy in the hierarchy Bouteldja describes. And she herself is unflinching in acknowledging this risk for herself, a risk she understands as tantamount to her own destruction. Exposed to the repeated equation of Jews and Zionism, the relentless claim that Israel is, as it itself proclaims, "the state of the Jewish people," along with the persistent affirmation that Zionism constitutes the liberation of all Jews, what Bouteldja fears is "the disappearance of my indifference toward you, the possible prelude to my internal ruin" (58). Indifference, of course, remains the twisted norm, where the separation of Muslim and Jew serves as a framing, and blinding, device. And it is what Bouteldja fears and resists.

Bouteldja elaborates on that indifference, on the disappearance of inextricable entanglements, in a poignant gesture in which she calls on the memory of Algerian Jews in particular (once again, the broader import of a local instance is clear enough). Here, again, the perspective is dual, recognizing loss—since what is at stake is both the Jewish memory of Algeria and the contemporary remembrance of Jewish presence in Algeria—and including the crucial role of France in this dynamic. "You can't ignore the fact that France made you French to tear you away from us, from your land, from your Arab-Berber identity [*votre arabo-ber-bérité*]. If I dare say so, from your Islamic identity [*votre islamité*]. Just as we have been dispossessed of you. If I dare say so, of our Jewish identity [*notre judéité*]. Incidentally, I can't think about North Africa without missing you. You left a void that we will never be able to fill, and for that I am inconsolable. Your alterity becomes more pronounced and your memory fades" (60).

In the intra-acting logic and illogic of a lost Jewish *islamité,* of a vanished Muslim *judéité,* we witness the undoing of the theologico-political history, which I traced in *The Jew, the Arab,* a history that has long associated and dissociated the Jewish question from the Muslim question. There is nostalgia in Bouteldja, yes, but the significance of such unsettling gestures as the one she performs has as much to do with the past as with the future. The question—or rather, the responses to the questions that occupy us in this volume and that organize Bouteldja's reflections—is underscored in a recurring thread of Bouteldja's book, which she draws from C. L. R. James, whereby history, and most particularly those events the West thinks of as defeats, along with the death and destruction the West itself has unleashed, must be reconsidered as a shared history. "If we invite you to share in Algerian independence and the victory in Dien Bien Phu," challenges Bouteldja, "would you agree to break your solidarity with your warmongering states?" (50). Just as James offered whites "the memory of his negro ancestors who rose against you" (50) Bouteldja might ask Americans to think of Vietnam as a victory rather than a defeat, a true victory for "freedom" (or at least its promise). She definitely asks of France to think of anticolonial struggles along such lines. Appealing to a universal solidarity that has yet to fully emerge, Bouteldja goes further. She also defies her addressee to reformulate the universality of the Holocaust. I would argue that, true to the perspective I have been describing, she seeks an understanding of the Holocaust as global, something she herself calls "a decolonial reading of the Nazi genocide—the Shoah" (62). This is less a new reading than one that has been reductively understood and consistently opposed under the heading of "the competition of victims." But the historical and geo-theologico-political link between the Holocaust and colonialism constitutes an inescapable, and undoubtedly planetary, chapter in the series of entanglements that binds the Jewish question and the Muslim question.

The paradox here is that the universal import of the Holocaust, its significance as a crime against humanity that must be acknowledged by all (along with the global obligation of memory and the recognition demanded of an equally global threat of anti-Semitism, which Bouteldja decries as the branding of "the indigenous mass with the seal of anti-Semitic infamy" [61]), is also, and in the same gesture, restricted to a particular—in fact, to an *exceptional*—understanding of its victims (that it is also a divided understanding is equally clear from the politics of Holocaust memory, inscribed at the center of Berlin and elsewhere by distinct and separate memorials). Thus any attempt to have slavery or colonialism recognized as crimes against humanity is immediately perceived as a threat to the uniqueness of the Holocaust. Bouteldja acknowledges the threat, the fear. "The risk of removing its singularity from the Nazi genocide is real," she writes, "and you would be right to point it out. The negationist tendency looms large with the anti-Semites" (63). Yet, in another version of the overall logic she scrutinizes, everything is as if Jews had to be the only representatives of the humanity against which the Nazi crime was perpetrated. And such (exceptional) humanity is not accessible to the "indigenous mass" that clamor for recognition of—or worse, reparations for—the crimes perpetrated against them. In the division between Nazism and colonialism, therefore, what is reinscribed is the enduring separation of the Jew, the Arab. There is found the true planetary dimension with which I began, as well as the lingering effect of a strange policy (written or hidden) that divides and rules, that separates and distinguishes among the collectives it fights, governs, or manages according to enduring theologico-political and colonial entanglements and arrangements, overt or covert (such division had of course begun to be undone in the work of Hannah Arendt, the significance of which was famously remarked upon by Aimé Césaire, Edward Said, and Amnon Raz-Krakotzkin, among others). Ah, but there is no peace in Bethlehem, lament the arms merchants. "I find it a remarkable irony," writes Talal Asad in a proximate spirit, "that up to about the end of the Second World War, if not later, European (or Christian) civilization was triumphantly declared to be the creator of the modern world but that now, confronted with a menacing future, it is more common to hear people talk about *humanity*'s self-destruction—as though the peasants and working classes of the world had the same responsibility for that future as the industrialists, politicians, military careerists, bankers, and arms manufacturers."[6] Like Bouteldja, Asad insists that the local has long become the global, and that what looked like circumscribed events have shared significance. What could it mean, then, to maintain distinctions between "questions" that have never been isolated from each other, as if the consequences could be faced elsewhere. Separating histories can hardly ensure a shared future. This is why Bouteldja is daringly, but necessarily, putting the Holocaust on the line. She seeks, against all too many odds, to draw a common future from a conception of history that insists on separations. The lesson could not be clearer, as we have already seen. And it involves, to begin with, the Jew, the Arab, the *islamité* of the Jews, and the *judéité* of the Muslims.

## Democracy against the State

I want to conclude by reciprocating, as it were, and elaborating, after Bouteldja's fashion, on the *islamité* of the Jews. I do so by invoking one of those striking Biblical moments, where the text lays out in the open that which it knows, and wants its readers to know, even as it inscribes the broader and insistent contours of a familiar denial. By way of background, I will say that I have been reminded of two thinkers who have thought about a democracy that is yet to come, one that orients Bouteldja as well, as the preceding pages should have made clear. At stake is, first, a *forgotten* democracy such as Nicole Loraux describes it (going back to Solon's Athens) and, second, a democracy against the state, to which Miguel Abensour attends (going back to Marx and Machiavelli).[7] For Solon, in Loraux's account, *stasis* (a word that, at the root of state and stance, of institution and constitution, conveys both the stability of the state and the instability of factions, hence its common translation as "civil war") is at the heart of democracy, historically at its root. Affirming, even fostering disagreement and dispute, democracy cannot but place the demos on the edge of war and conflict. There is no democracy without factions, parties at odds with each other. How far does the antagonism go? This is what (Greek) democracy knows and what it also forgets. In a fascinating instance of enforcing a retro-prospective memory, Solon acknowledged the constitutive (and unmaking) role of stasis as civil war when he made a law that, after the end of the war, would harshly punish anyone who had not taken a stance, not chosen a side.

In a distinct but related manner, Abensour reads democracy as that which undoes the state; as that which, from the first, abolishes the profoundly undemocratic distinction upon which the modern state is based: the distinction between citizen and noncitizen. Democracy, in this perspective, is not a separation but a kind of originary contest, an unstable state of affairs: stasis, and not a state. Otherwise put (and here I am also relying on Dimitris Vardoulakis's elaborations[8]), it is from stasis as democracy, the conflictual and agonistic multitude, that collective institutions emerge, the state being one among them (and a destructive one at that). To think democratically is therefore to think beyond the distinction between citizen and noncitizen, while recognizing—remembering—dispute, conflict, stasis. Now, much as the Greeks sought to forget stasis as the necessary corollary, the constitutive undoing of politics and of the "democratic state" (that great oxymoron, according to Abensour), I want to illustrate the way the Bible insists on remembering what its readers would rather forget, commanding a memory of that which it itself inscribes and denies. Consider, then, in the spirit (but not the state) of democracy, how something akin to stasis operates in the following lines.

> When the Lord your God brings you into the land that he swore to your fathers, Abraham, Isaac, and Jacob, to assign to you great and flourishing cities that you did not build, houses full of all good things that you did not fill, hewn cisterns that you do not hew, vineyards and olive groves that you did not plant—and you eat your fill, take heed that you do not forget the Lord who freed you from the land of Egypt, the house of bondage. Revere only the Lord your God and worship Him alone, and swear only by His name. Do not follow other gods, any gods of the people about you. For the Lord your God in your midst is an impassioned God, lest the anger of the Lord your God blaze forth against you and He wipe you off the face of the earth.[9]

What is remarkable about this passage is that—for better or for worse—it describes a familiar promised land. (Is it Israel/Palestine or France, or America, that is here described? Palestinian labor, colonial immigration, or Atlantic slavery?) It acknowledges gods and inhabitants, builders and tillers, "the people about you" that dwell in the land. Surely, the distinction, even separation, is starkly inscribed between the members of the collective placed under the divine injunction and those upon whose work and life they depend, the fruit of whose labor they enjoy. Yet the privileged collective is clearly and insistently reminded of its historical and material (and theological) dependence, of the debt it has incurred with those who built the dwelling and planted the fields, those who made possible the very conditions of their existence, those who are still "about you." Looking toward the past and the present, the divine injunction functions therefore as a constant reminder of past and of present. It prescribes a memory and it constitutes a future as well. Indeed, if, as Loraux showed, Athenian democracy was predicated on the forgetting of stasis, one can see a distinct practice of remembrance here at work. For to remember God is to remember the "beings of the earth" (as Donna Haraway has it[10]), those whose labor and achievements rendered, and render still, the ancient Hebrews' existence possible. Along with the covenant, though, memory, the memory of God, constitutes a promise that is also a threat, a threat that reminds us of the beings of the earth, yes, but also of the earth itself, of the planet: a world without us, as it were. For the divine covenant is famously far from unconditional, and it rather requires what Haraway calls "unexpected collaborations and combinations,"[11] their activation and their interruption, but in any case, the practice and the consciousness of a drastic, and obviously violent, finitude. A different kind of memory, and a different kind of democracy. It is as if the Bible sought to remind its readers of a possibility articulated, once again, by Bouteldja. "To be honest, between us, everything is still possible. ... We have a common destiny in the same way that we potentially have a common political future" (67). Alluding to the diasporic and transnational—planetary—dimensions of the Jew, the Muslim, Bouteldja goes on to add that "we have this in common that we do not make up the legitimate bodies of the nation" (68). One might say:

of the state. That is why, for her, "we stand before a fool's game, in which we are the celebrities playing the main roles. Jews and Arabs, those terrible and turbulent children who exhaust themselves reconciling the good Christian souls. While the main actor is white: the West" (69). Bouteldja concludes with an offer—democracy against the state—and it is one that would take seriously the divine injunction I quoted earlier. It is also one that questions the ambiguous exceptionality that continues to mark the separate questions. In response, then, Bouteldja offers a different question. "You are losing your historical friends," she writes. "You are still in the ghetto. Why don't we get out of there together?" (72). ■

# Note on Contributors

**Gil Anidjar** is professor in the Department of Religion and the Department of Middle Eastern, South Asian, and African Studies at Columbia University. He is author of, among other things, *The Jew, the Arab: A History of the Enemy* (2003), and *Blood: A Critique of Christianity* (2014).

**Jonathan Boyarin** is professor of anthropology and director of Jewish studies at Cornell University. He is author of numerous articles and books, including *The Unconverted Self: Jews, Indians, and the Identity of Christian Europe* (2009) and, with Martin Land, *Time and Human Language Now* (2008).

**Holly Case** is professor of history at Brown University. She recently published *The Age of Questions; or, A First Attempt at an Aggregate History of the Eastern, Social, Woman, American, Jewish, Polish, Bullion, Tuberculosis, and Many Other Questions over the Nineteenth Century, and Beyond* (2018).

**Joyce Dalsheim** is a cultural anthropologist and associate professor in the Department of Global Studies at the University of North Carolina at Charlotte. She is author of *Unsettling Gaza: Secular Liberalism, Radical Religion, and the Israeli Settlement Project* (2011), *Producing Spoilers: Peacemaking and the Production of Enmity in a Secular Age* (2014), and, most recently, *Israel Has a Jewish Problem: Self-Determination as Self-Elimination* (2019).

**Martin Land** is a physicist who teaches at Hadassah Academic College, in Jerusalem. In addition to publishing many articles in his field, Land has collaborated with Jonathan Boyarin on several publications, including *Time and Human Language Now* (2008) and *Jews and the Ends of Theory* (2018).

**Gregory Starrett** is professor of anthropology at the University of North Carolina at Charlotte. He is author of *Putting Islam to Work: Education, Politics, and Religious Transformation in Egypt* (1998) and coeditor, with Eleanor Abdella Doumato, of *Teaching Islam: Textbooks and Religion in the Middle East* (2007). He previously collaborated with Joyce Dalsheim on their coauthored article, "Time and the Spectral Other: Demonstrating against 'Unite the Right 2'" (2019), in *Anthropology Today*.

Although their voices are not represented in this brief volume, we would like to acknowledge the contributions to our conversations in Denver and at Cornell University of the following people: Nadia Abu El-Haj, Aomar Boum, Virginia Dominguez, Grant Farred, Neil Levi, Tracy McNulty, Irene Silverblatt, and Enzo Traverso. We look forward to continuing and expanding this work.

We are grateful to Paul Fleming, director of the Society for the Humanities at Cornell, and the university's Jewish Studies Program for cosponsoring the spring 2018 workshop.

# Notes

### Introduction

1.  Augustine, *The City of God*, trans. Marcus Dods (New York: Modern Library, 2000), 657.

2.  Augustine, *Tractatus adversus Iudaeos* (Treatise against the Jews), quoted in Jeremy Cohen, *Living Letters of the Law: Ideas of the Jew in Medieval Christianity* (Berkeley: University of California Press, 1999), 40.

3.  Gelya Frank, "Jews, Multiculturalism, and Boasian Anthropology," *American Anthropologist* 99, no. 4 (1997): 731–45; Ronald Schechter, *Obstinate Hebrews: Representations of Jews in France, 1715–1815* (Berkeley: University of California Press, 2003), 7.

4.  John Lie, "The Structure of Afterthought," *Identities* 19, no. 4 (2012): 544–55.

5.  Joyce Dalsheim, "Theory for Praxis: Peacemaking, Cunning Recognition, and the Constitution of Enmity," *Social Analysis* 57, no. 2 (2013): 59–80.

6.  Robert Launay, *Savages, Romans, and Despots: Thinking about Others from Montaigne to Herder* (Chicago: University of Chicago Press, 2018), 210–11.

7.  Daniel Boyarin, "The Christian Invention of Judaism: The Theodosian Empire and the Rabbinic Refusal of Religion," *Representations* 85, no. 1 (2004): 21–57.

8.  Jonathan Boyarin, *Thinking in Jewish* (Chicago: University of Chicago Press, 1996).

### Chapter Two

1.  Richard J. Bernstein, *Hannah Arendt and the Jewish Question* (Cambridge, MA: MIT Press, 1996), xi–xii.

2.  See Holly Case, *The Age of Questions; or, A First Attempt at an Aggregate History of the Eastern, Social, Woman, American, Jewish, Polish, Bullion, Tuberculosis, and Many Other Questions over the Nineteenth Century, and Beyond* (Princeton, NJ: Princeton University Press, 2018). Readers should refer to the book for additional documentation regarding points discussed in this chapter.

3. Leo Tolstoy, "The Non-Acting," in *The Complete Works of Count Tolstoy*, vol. 23, trans. Leo Wiener (Boston: Dana Estes, 1905), 50.

4. Lyof N. Tolstoï, *Anna Karenina*, trans. Nathan Haskell Dole (New York: Thomas Y. Crowell, 1899), 340–41, 344–47, 384–88.

5. From John M. Ziman, *Puzzles, Problems, and Enigmas: Occasional Pieces on the Human Aspects of Science* (Cambridge: Cambridge University Press, 1981), 34.

6. Norman Davies, *God's Playground: A History of Poland, 1795 to the Present* (New York: Columbia University Press, 2005), 11.

7. "Resurrexi," *Evening Star* of the *Thames Star*, December 20, 1881.

8. W. P., "A Lament for Romance," *Mayfair Magazine* (London), December 1883.

9. Alexis de Tocqueville, *Œuvres complètes*, vol. 7, *Nouvelle correspondance* (Paris: Michel Lévy frères, 1866), 313. De Tocqueville added that Napoléon once said this to Lafayette.

10. Cited in Musa Gümüş, "Namık Kemâl'e Göre 'Şark Meselesi' ve Osmanlı Devleti'ni Cöküşe Götüren Sorunlar" [The "Eastern question" and other questions leading to the collapse of the Ottoman state, according to Namık Kemal], in *History Studies—International Journal of History*, Ortadoğu Özel Sayısı [Special Middle East(ern) issue] (2010): 148.

11. See Bruno Bauer, *The Jewish Problem*, trans. Helen Lederer (Cincinnati, OH: Hebrew Union College–Jewish Institute of Religion, 1958).

12. Mary Gluck, *The Invisible Jewish Budapest: Metropolitan Culture at the Fin De Siècle* (Madison: University of Wisconsin Press, 2016), 40.

13. *Oxford English Dictionary*, 2nd ed. (1989), s.v. "question, n."

14. Christopher Hitchens, *Hitch-22* (New York: Twelve, 2010), e-book.

15. F. M. Dostoievsky, *The Diary of a Writer*, trans. Boris Brasol (New York: George Braziller, 1954), 428.

16. Jacob Toury, "'The Jewish Question': A Semantic Approach," Leo Baeck Institute Year Book 11, no. 1 (1966): 89–90.

17. Ibid., 92.

18. Ibid., 100.

19. Ibid., 101.

20. "To Correspondents," *Times* (London), April 23, 1830.

21. My translation. Erik Molnár, "Zsidókérdés Magyarországon" [The Jewish question in Hungary], in *Zsidókérdés, Asszimiláció, Antiszemitizmus: Tanulmányok a Zsidókérdésről a Huszadik Századi Magyarországon* [Jewish question, assimilation, antisemitism: Studies on the Jewish question in twentieth-century Hungary], ed. Péter Hanák (Budapest: Gondolat, 1984), 121.

22. Richard S. Levy, *Antisemitism: A Historical Encyclopedia of Prejudice and Persecution* (Santa Barbara, CA: ABC-CLIO, 2005), 377.

23. Benjamin Disraeli, *Tancred; or, The New Crusade*, vol. 1 (Paris: A. and W. Galignani, 1847), 267.

24. George Augustus Sala, "The Strange Behaviour of Mr. Apostolo," *Belgravia Annual*, December 25, 1877.

25. See Jacob Toury's work, discussed above, which notes that the term appeared in English in the mid-eighteenth century; but it was not until the nineteenth century that the term came into common usage. For an example of dating the origin of the Jewish question to the emergence of Judaism, see P. Horowitz, *The Jewish Question and Zionism* (London: Ernest Benn, 1927).

26. Theodor Herzl, *The Jewish State: An Attempt at a Modern Solution of the Jewish Question*, trans. Sylvie D'Avigdor, trans. rev. Jacob De Haas (1896; New York: Maccabæan, 1904), 3.

27. Heinrich von Treitschke, "A Word about Our Jewry," in *The Jew in the Modern World: A Documentary History*, ed. Paul R. Mendes-Flohr and Jehuda Reinharz (New York: Oxford University Press, 1980), 281.

28. Cited in Alex Bein, *The Jewish Question: Biography of a World Problem* (New York: Herzl Press, 1990), 20.

29. Leonid Andreyev, "The First Step," in *The Shield*, ed. Maxim Gorky, Leonid Andreyev, and Fyodor Sologub, trans. A. Yarmolinsky (New York: Knopf, 1917), 23.

30. My translation. Leonhard Weydmann, *Die Fragen unserer bewegten Zeit im Lichte des Evangeliums und mit beständiger Rücksicht auf die Urtheile der Reformatoren betrachtet* [The questions of our tumultuous time in light of the Gospel and with constant consideration for the judgments of the Reformers] (Frankfurt am Main: Heinr. Ludw. Brönner Verlag, 1834), 1–2.

31. Robert Cecil, Marquess of Salisbury, *Essays by the Late Marquess of Salisbury* (London: John Murray, 1905), 3.

32. Bein, *Jewish Question*, 21–22.

33. My translation. Edmondo de Amicis, "Úvahy o socialné otázce" [Reflections on the social question], *Athenaeum* (October 15, 1892), 10–12.

34. Herzl, *Jewish State*, 55.

35. Stephanie Laudyn [Stefanja Laudynowa], *A World Problem: Jews—Poland—Humanity; A Psychological and Historical Study*, part 1, trans. A. J. Zieliński and W. K. ... (Chicago: American Catalogue Printing, 1920), 5–6.

36. Ernest Mandel, "Jewish Question since World War II," *Fourth International* 8, no. 4 (1947): 109–13. Available at www.marxists.org/archive/mandel/1946/07/jews.htm.

37. Jean Lahovary, *The Jewish Question in Roumania* (London: Raggett, 1906), 30–32, 47.

38. Walter Scott, *The Eastern or Jewish Question Considered: And, What the Bible Says About Coming Events* (London: Alfred Holness, 1882), 3.

39. *Brandeis on Zionism: A Collection of Addresses and Statements by Louis D. Brandeis* (Union, NJ: Lawbook Exchange, 1999), 26.

40. Adolf Grabowsky, *Die polnische Frage* [The Polish question] (Berlin: C. Heymann, 1916), 3–4.

41. From a conversation between Hitler and Molotov, November 12, 1940. Andreas Hillgruber, *Staatsmänner und Diplomaten bei Hitler* [Statesman and diplomats with Hitler], vol. 1 (Frankfurt am Main: Bernard u. Graefe, 1967), 299. Also, in a 1939 speech to the Reichstag, Hitler vowed to "push for a solution to, among many others, the Jewish problem." Adolf Hitler, *Hitler: Reden und Proklamationen, 1932–1945* [Hitler: Speeches and proclamations, 1932–1945], ed. Max Domarus (Leonberg: Pamminger, 1988), 1058.

42. Albert Gates, "The Jewish Problem after Hitler: Palestine and the Fourth International," *New International* 13, no. 7 (1947): 206–10. Available at www.marxists.org/history/etol/writers/glotzer/1947/09/jewishprob.html.

**Chapter Three**

1. Raymond Ruyer, *Neofinalism*, trans. Alyosha Edlebi (Minneapolis: University of Minnesota Press, 2016), 8.

2. Masha Gessen, "When Does a Watershed Become a Sex Panic?" *New Yorker*, November 14, 2017, www.newyorker.com/news/our-columnists/when-does-a-watershed-become-a-sex-panic; "Sex, Consent, and the Dangers of 'Misplaced Scale,'" *New Yorker*, November 27, 2017, www.newyorker.com/news/our-columnists/sex-consent-dangers-of-misplaced-scale.

3. Gershom Scholem, "Toward an Understanding of the Messianic Idea in Judaism," trans. Michael A. Meyer, in *The Messianic Idea in Judaism and Other Essays on Jewish Spirituality* (New York: Schocken Books, 1971), 52.

4. Timothy Snyder, *On Tyranny: Twenty Lessons from the Twentieth Century* (New York: Tim Duggan, 2017).

5. In the lunchroom of my yeshiva on the Lower East Side today, I saw a man whom I did not recognize sitting and eating his lunch. Next to him on the table lay a book with the English-language title *Close Reading Strategies for Complex Texts*. Apparently, however, it wasn't designed to assist the student of the Talmud: www.sadlier.com/school/close-reading-strategies-for-complex-texts.

6. Sergey Dolgopolski, "Jews, in Theory," in *Jews and the Ends of Theory*, ed. Shai Ginsburg, Martin Land and Jonathan Boyarin (New York: Fordham University Press, 2018).

7. Rana Mitter, "Barbarians Out!," review of *Out of China: How the Chinese Ended the Era of Western Domination*, by Robert Bickers, *New York Review of Books*, December 7, 2017, www.nybooks.com/articles/2017/12/07/out-of-china-barbarians.

8. John F. Kennedy, "Address on the First Anniversary of the Alliance for Progress," in *Public Papers of the Presidents: John F. Kennedy; 1962* (Washington, DC: United States Government Printing Office, 1963), 223.

9. Dave Boyer, "Michael Bloomberg: Donald Trump a 'Con Man,'" *Washington Times*, July 27, 2016, www.washingtontimes.com/news/2016/jul/27/michael-bloomberg-donald-trump-con-man/.

## Chapter Four

1. Quoted in Elliot R. Wolfson, "Suffering Time: Maharal's Influence on Hasidic Perspectives on Temporality," *Kabbalah: Journal for the Study of Jewish Mystical Texts* 44 (2019): 9.

2. Walter Benjamin, "Theses on the Philosophy of History," in *Illuminations*, ed. Hannah Arendt, trans. Harry Zohn (New York: Schocken Books, 1968), 257 (Thesis 8).

3. Jacques Derrida, *Specters of Marx: The State of the Debt, the Work of Mourning, and the New International*, trans. Peggy Kamuf (New York: Routledge, 2006), 96–97.

4. Joan W. Scott, "On Free Speech and Academic Freedom" (remarks given on receiving the Talcott Parsons Prize from the American Academy of Arts and Sciences, Cambridge, MA, April 6, 2017, www.amacad.org/news/free-speech-and-academic-freedom).

5. Joan Wallach Scott page on Institute for Advanced Study website ("Scholars" section), accessed April 21, 2020, www.ias.edu/scholars/scott.

6. Karl Marx and Friedrich Engels, "Manifesto of the Communist Party," in *The Marx-Engels Reader*, 2nd ed., ed. Robert C. Tucker (New York: W. W. Norton, 1978), 475–77.

7. *Selections from the Prison Notebooks of Antonio Gramsci*, ed. and trans. Quintin Hoare and Geoffrey Nowell-Smith (New York: International Publishers, 1971), 276.

8. Thomas Chatterton Williams, "The French Origins of 'You Will Not Replace Us,'" *New Yorker*, November 27, 2017, www.newyorker.com/magazine/2017/12/04/the-french-origins-of-you-will-not-replace-us.

9. Joyce Dalsheim, "Theory for Praxis: Peacemaking, Cunning Recognition, and the Constitution of Enmity," *Theory, Culture & Society* 57, no. 2 (2013): 59–80.

10. Gregory Starrett, "When Theory Is Data: Coming to Terms with 'Culture' as a Way of Life," in *Explaining Culture Scientifically*, ed. Melissa J. Brown, 264–85 (Seattle: University of Washington Press, 2008).

11. Webb Keane, *Christian Moderns: Freedom and Fetish in the Mission Encounter* (Berkeley: University of California Press, 2007).

12. Irene Silverblatt, *Modern Inquisitions: Peru and the Colonial Origins of the Civilized World* (Durham, NC: Duke University Press, 2004).

13. Cynthia M. Baker, *Jew* (New Brunswick, NJ: Rutgers University Press, 2017), 7.

14. Michael Löwy, *Fire Alarm: Reading Walter Benjamin's "On the Concept of History"* (London: Verso, 2016), 28.

15. Hannah Arendt, *The Origins of Totalitarianism* (New York: Harcourt, Brace, 1968), 291.

16. Susan Buck-Morss, "Comment on Bunzl," in *Anti-Semitism and Islamophobia: Hatreds Old and New in Europe*, ed. Matti Bunzl, 95 (Chicago: Prickly Paradigm, 2007).

17. Baker, *Jew*, 4.

18. Ilan Halevi, *A History of the Jews: Ancient and Modern* (London: Zed, 1987), 1.

19. Joyce Dalsheim, *Israel Has a Jewish Problem: Self-Determination as Self-Elimination* (Oxford: Oxford University Press, 2019).

20. Benjamin, "Theses on the Philosophy of History," 257 (Thesis 8).

21. Ibid., 255 (Thesis 5).

22. Ibid. 257 (Thesis 8). Translation modified.

23. Jonathan Boyarin, *Thinking in Jewish* (Chicago: University of Chicago Press, 1996).

24. Löwy, *Fire Alarm*, 91.

25. Max Weinreich, *History of the Yiddish Language*, trans. Schlomo Noble (Chicago: University of Chicago Press, 1980).

**Chapter Five**

1. Karen Barad, *Meeting the Universe Halfway: Quantum Physics and the Entanglement of Matter and Meaning* (Durham, NC: Duke University Press, 2007).

2. Gil Anidjar, *The Jew, the Arab: A History of the Enemy* (Stanford, CA: Stanford University Press, 2003).

3. Houria Bouteldja, *Whites, Jews, and Us: Toward a Politics of Revolutionary Love*, trans. Rachel Valinsky (South Pasadena, CA: Semiotext(e), 2017). All subsequent citations refer to this edition and appear in-text and only include page numbers.

4. Yuri Slezkine, *The Jewish Century* (Princeton, NJ: Princeton University Press, 2004).

5. Robert Meister, *After Evil: A Politics of Human Rights* (New York: Columbia University Press, 2010), 179.

6. Talal Asad, *Secular Translations: Nation-State, Modern Self, and Calculative Reason* (New York: Columbia University Press, 2018), 10.

7. Nicole Loraux, *The Divided City: On Memory and Forgetting in Ancient Athens*, trans. Corinne Pache and Jeff Fort (New York: Zone Books, 2001); Miguel Abensour, *Democracy against the State: Marx and the Machiavellian Moment*, trans. Max Blechman and Martin Breaugh (Cambridge: Polity Press, 2011).

8. Dimitris Vardoulakis, *Stasis before the State: Nine Theses on Agonistic Democracy* (New York: Fordham University Press, 2017).

9. Deut. 6: 10–15. *Tanakh: The Holy Scriptures* (Philadelphia: Jewish Publication Society, 1985).

10. Donna J. Haraway, *Staying with the Trouble: Making Kin in the Chthulucene* (Durham, NC: Duke University Press, 2016), 2.

11. Ibid., 4.

Also available from Prickly Paradigm Press:

*continued*

*continued*